Research Report

Air Force Officer Accession Planning

Addressing Key Gaps in Meeting Career Field Academic Degree Requirements for Nonrated Officers

Lisa M. Harrington, Tara L. Terry

RAND Project AIR FORCE

Prepared for the United States Air Force
Approved for public release; distribution unlimited

RAND CORPORATION

For more information on this publication, visit www.rand.org/t/RR1099

Library of Congress Cataloging-in-Publication Data is available for this publication.

ISBN: 978-0-8330-9123-9

Published by the RAND Corporation, Santa Monica, Calif.

Preface

The goal of the Air Force officer accession process is to ensure the Air Force obtains and classifies officers with the qualifications, knowledge, skills, and attributes to perform various Air Force missions in particular career fields. Key to this goal for nonrated officers is establishing and enforcing academic degree requirements. Over the course of our research, we uncovered gaps in line officer accession processes that currently undermine or have the potential to undermine successfully meeting career field education requirements. This document summarizes our work to identify these gaps, assess their effect on the accession process, and offer recommendations for correcting or mitigating these gaps.

The research reported here was sponsored by SAF/AQX Acquisition Integration and AF/A1P Force Management Policy and conducted within the Manpower, Personnel, and Training Program of RAND Project AIR FORCE as part of a fiscal year 2014 project entitled "STEM Officer Accessions."

RAND Project AIR FORCE

RAND Project AIR FORCE (PAF), a division of the RAND Corporation, is the U.S. Air Force's federally funded research and development center for studies and analyses. PAF provides the Air Force with independent analyses of policy alternatives affecting the development, employment, combat readiness, and support of current and future air, space, and cyber forces. Research is conducted in four programs: Force Modernization and Employment; Manpower, Personnel, and Training; Resource Management; and Strategy and Doctrine. The research reported here was prepared under contract FA7014-06-C-0001.

Additional information about PAF is available on our website:
http://www.rand.org/paf/

Table of Contents

Appendixes

Figures

Tables

Summary

Background

The Air Force commissions thousands of officers each year. Three sources provide the vast majority of these officers: the U.S. Air Force Academy (USAFA), Air Force Reserve Officer Training Corps (AFROTC), and Officer Training School. Typically, about 3,000 of these newly commissioned officers become what are called *line officers*. Within the line category, they subdivide into two additional categories, rated and nonrated. Broadly speaking, line officers exercise command authority and lead the combat and combat support elements of the service. *Nonline officers* are specialists, such as doctors and chaplains. Rated officers serve in flying assignments as pilots, pilots of remotely piloted aircraft, combat systems officers, and air battle managers. The nonrated officers serve in assignments related to such specialties as logistic, maintenance, and personnel.

The Air Force spends considerable effort matching the skills and abilities of incoming officers with career field assignments. It uses the type of academic degree the newly commissioned officers have earned as one proxy for the skills and abilities desired for specific career field assignments. A multitude of staff and field activities manage the accession process to ensure the Air Force obtains officers qualified to perform various Air Force missions in particular career fields. Key to this goal is satisfying the academic degree requirements that functional authorities and career field managers (CFMs) have established.

Purpose

Given the importance of academic degrees in the determination of career field requirements and assignments, it is important for the Air Force to ensure that the types of degrees it uses to guide the assignment process deliver the skills and abilities it seeks and that the system in place delivers individuals to the assignments that most benefit from their academic backgrounds. This is particularly important for officers commissioned from the USAFA or through the AFROTC scholarship program because of the expense of these programs. The Air Force asked the Project AIR FORCE (PAF) to investigate, document, and assess current processes for obtaining line officer accessions with appropriate degrees, identifying any gaps in what the Air Force wants to achieve with its accession processes and recommending any improvements needed to these processes. This document summarizes our analysis of the Air Force's programs and processes for matching officers with career field assignments. It focuses primarily on line officers being assigned to nonrated career fields.

Scope

The goals and constraints of the research sponsors shaped the analytic approach used in this research. Given their limited time frame and the resources they could dedicate to changing policies and practices, they requested that we suggest incremental improvements to the existing processes for identifying academic degree needs, evaluating the extent that academic needs are met in classification, understanding aggregate degree needs, and applying AFROTC scholarships to meet the needs. The sponsors were not open to, for example, significantly changing how academic degree requirements were defined, or to requiring accession sources to gather, maintain and report additional information on cadets requiring classification. Given the number of nonrated officers classified annually, the sponsors emphasized that they needed a method that was not overly labor intensive.

The participation of the approximately 20 nonrated line functional managers and CFMs was key in this effort. Within the Air Force human resource structure, these individuals are responsible for ensuring that their specialties are equipped, developed, and sustained to provide Air Force capabilities (AFI 36-2640). Any proposed changes to the accession process need to apply to the wide range of specialties and to recognize CFMs' role in reviewing and validating academic degree requirements.

Finally, research has been and continues to be conducted on the appropriate measures for assessing cadet quality, including leadership ability, potential performance, and how to include these quality measures in the classification process. The research sponsor asked us to focus on academic degree considerations.

Findings and Recommendations

Over the course of our research, we uncovered gaps in line officer accession processes that currently undermine or have the potential to undermine successful meeting of career field education requirements. In summary, these gaps and our recommendations are as follows:

There is no agreement across the service on the role of academic degrees in qualifying an individual for an Air Force specialty. We found disagreements on the resources that should be expended to fulfill career field education desires. We recommend that AF/A1, responsible for providing the human capital for Air Force missions, clearly state the Air Force philosophy on establishing education requirements for Air Force officers. This policy should be communicated across the Air Force to the functional authorities and CFMs who are responsible for setting education requirements and to organizations supplying officer accessions.

There is no feedback mechanism for determining whether education, quality, and preference goals are being met for individual career fields. We found that no analysis was being performed after the yearly classification of USAFA and AFROTC cadets to determine the extent to which career field academic degree requirements were being met. We developed an approach for scoring the effectiveness of the classification and applied it to the fiscal year 2014 classification results. In addition, we recommend creating feedback loops to ensure the Accession and Training Management Division (AF/A1PT) and CFMs are aware of degree requirements that cannot be met so they can mitigate the consequences. The Air Force personnel organization and sources of commission can work to avoid these shortages in the out-years.

No evidence-based methodologies exist for establishing education requirements for entry into an Air Force specialty. As we worked with CFMs to understand how they establish career field education requirements, we discovered that they lacked the tools to tie key abilities officers require to the degrees that best provide these capabilities. We developed a survey methodology for CFMs to administer to determine the capabilities best learned by seeking particular degrees for clusters of jobs within a career field. We recommend that the Directorate of Force Management Policy (AF/A1P) establish a repository for the survey and encourage CFMs to administer these surveys to samples of their officers as their career fields change; as career fields are merged or split; or as the required knowledge, skills, abilities, and other characteristics for job clusters change. We also recommend that AF/A1P establish a process for validating and revalidating education requirements periodically. This process will help militate against expending unnecessary resources in recruiting and accessing officers with academic degrees that are not needed but that are difficult to recruit.

Documentation formats for stating education requirements for Air Force specialties are vague. We evaluated the current method for documenting and communicating career field education requirements at various points in the officer accession process and determined that a new framework for documentation could better meet career field needs. We recommend that AF/A1P mandate this framework as the standard for all nonrated career field education requirements. This method of documentation clearly states priorities and desired percentages of degree types and specifies particular degree types. We also recommend that AF/A1P use this framework to establish optimal targets by career field and academic degree type. These targets can reorient the degree types that the sources of commission produce over time to better meet career field degree requirements.

The linkages between career field academic degree requirements and incentives (such as AFROTC scholarships) for individuals to pursue the degrees are imperfect. We also examined AFROTC scholarships to determine whether they provided incentives to cadets to pursue degrees required by career fields. We found that scholarships do not necessarily align with career field education requirements and that production of particular degree types will need to increase as degree programs and career fields change. Most important, we recommend that AFROTC and AF/A1P gather sufficient data and metrics to assess the effect of scholarship dollars and the value of scholarships in obtaining accessions with needed degrees.

Recommendations for Future Research

The constraints on the sponsor limited the research approaches we could employ. We recommend that additional approaches be considered for future research. First, we would recommend investigating ways to capture more-detailed academic degree information in classifications beyond the academic major, including academic minors, semester hours, and quality of institutions. Second, we recommend considering a more-flexible (and likely more-complicated) approach to the education matrices to account for more-diverse distributions of academic degrees. Third, we recommend additional investigations into methods for determining academic degree requirements. Fourth, we recommend additional testing of optimization solutions for aggregate nonrated line academic degree requirements, including investigating the best ways to express objectives and constraints. Also, given the current range of uncertainty in career field requirements and the potential degrees cadets earn each year, such methods as robust optimization (which provides the best performing solution against all possible outcomes in the uncertainty range[1]) should be investigated.

---

[1] See, for example Ben-Tal, 2009.

Acknowledgments

We would like to thank several people in the Air Force for their direction and guidance in developing and conducting this research. First and foremost, we thank our sponsor, David "Sammy" Slade for supporting our work and getting the high-level visibility our ideas needed to spark change. We would also like to thank Tina Strickland, Lt Col Jonelle Eychner, Richard Engle, and Maj Mark Cipolla from AF/A1PT for providing us with direction and contact information with regard to the participants in the officer accession process and including us in several CFM forums. We would like to thank all the participating offices for their willingness to share their knowledge regarding their roles and responsibilities in the officer accession process—AF/A3O, AF/A1P, AF/A1M, USAFA, Holm Center, Air Force Recruiting Service, AFROTC, and Air Force Personnel Center—and the CFMs who spent time with us to learn how to better provide for their accession education requirements. We would especially like to thank Sharon Restivo (recently retired from Air Force Personnel Center) for her patience in answering all our questions, Col (ret.) Frederick Guendel (AFROTC Deputy Registrar) for his consistent willingness to explain each aspect of AFROTC, ranging from each scholarship program to the Professional Officer Course selection process to AFROTC roles and responsibilities within the officer accession conference, and for patiently explaining the rationale for many AFROTC policies, and Col Todd Taylor (current AFROTC Deputy Registrar) for providing us with updated scholarship data.

We would also like to thank several people at RAND, including William Canny, who conducted some initial interviews regarding officer accessions, Sandra Petitjean for her quick work on the graphics in this document, Jerry Sollinger for his help in organizing and communicating our results, Al Robbert for his suggestions on how to best model accession targets, and Ray Conley and Lara Schmidt for their support and comments. The contributions of these individuals greatly improved the quality of the document. We also thank the reviewers, Al Robbert and Paul Davis, for helping us refine our focus and better shape our message resulting in a clearer, stronger report.

Abbreviations

AF/A1P	Deputy Chief of Staff for Manpower, Personnel and Services, Directorate of Force Management Policy
AF/A1M	Deputy Chief of Staff for Manpower, Personnel and Services, Directorate of Manpower, Organization & Resources
AF/A3O	Director of Operations and Readiness
ABM	air battle manager
AETC	Air Education and Training Command
AF/A3OI	Deputy Chief of Staff Operations, Force Integration Division
AF/A1PPR	Deputy Chief of Staff for Manpower, Personnel and Services, Military Force Policy Division, Rated Issues
AF/A1MP	Deputy Chief of Staff for Manpower, Personnel and Services, Program Development Division
AF/A1MR	Deputy Chief of Staff for Manpower, Personnel and Services, Requirements Division
AF/A1PF	Deputy Chief of Staff for Manpower, Personnel and Services, Force Management Division
AF/A1PT	Deputy Chief of Staff for Manpower, Personnel and Services, Accession and Training Management Division
AFOCD	Air Force Officer Classification Directory
AFPC	Air Force Personnel Center
AFROTC	Air Force Reserve Officer Training Corps
AFRS	Air Force Recruiting Service
AFS	Air Force specialty
AFSC	Air Force specialty code
AU	Air University
CFM	career field manager
CIP	Classification of Instructional Programs
CSO	combat systems officer
FA	functional authority
FY	fiscal year
FYDP	future years defense program
HQ	headquarters
ICSP	in-college scholarship program
IE	industrial engineering
KSAO	knowledge, skills, abilities, and other characteristics

MPES	Manpower Programming and Execution System
OAC	officer accession conference
OR	operations research
OTS	Officer Training School
PAF	Project AIR FORCE
PGL	program guidance letter
POC	Professional Officer Course
ROI	return on investment
RPA	remotely piloted aircraft
SOC	source of commission
STEM	science, technology, engineering, and mathematics
TPR	trained personnel requirement
USAFA	U.S. Air Force Academy
USAFA/A5/8/9	U.S. Air Force Academy, Directorate of Strategic Plan and Programs, Requirements, Assessments and Analyses
USAFA/A1A	U.S. Air Force Academy, Cadet Personnel Office

1. Introduction

Pathways to Air Force Commissions

Those wishing to become an Air Force officer can do so by following one of four paths: attending the U.S. Air Force Academy (USAFA), joining the Air Force Reserve Officer Training Corps (AFROTC) at a civilian institution, attending Officer Training School (OTS), and obtaining a direct commission.

The Air Force Academy

USAFA is the Air Force counterpart of the U.S. Military Academy at West Point and the Naval Academy at Annapolis. Typically, after four years, each USAFA graduate obtains a bachelor of science degree in a major of his or her choosing from a variety of degree programs offered at the academy. About 60 percent of the cadets complete majors in science and engineering; the other 40 percent graduate in the social sciences and humanities (USAF, 2004).[1] Students attending USAFA receive tuition, books, room and board, and a monthly stipend. Academy graduates incur a five-year active-duty service obligation.

Air Force Reserve Officer Training Corps

A cadet in AFROTC attends a civilian college or university and takes courses taught by the AFROTC detachment based either at the same institution or one nearby. With 144 detachments, AFROTC is the largest source of commissioned officers for the Air Force and is designed to recruit, educate, and commission officer candidates based on the needs of the Air Force. The Air Force relies heavily on AFROTC to produce STEM-degree graduates. After successfully completing all AFROTC requirements and obtaining a bachelor's degree in a major of their choosing, AFROTC cadets are commissioned as Air Force officers. AFROTC offers several different scholarships to aid students and to influence academic degree production to meet the academic needs of the career fields (discussed in Section 7). AFROTC cadets receive stipends once they enter their junior year and must serve four years on active duty.

Officer Training School

OTS trains college graduates (some of whom are enlisted personnel in the Air Force) and commissions them as second lieutenants in a nine-week program. OTS accession requirements

[1] Since all USAFA cadets are required to take core courses in science, mathematics, and engineering, all cadets graduate with bachelor of science degrees even if they major in fields other than in science, technology, engineering, and mathematics (STEM), such as the humanities and social sciences.

and accession production fluctuate in response to differences between projected and actual USAFA and AFROTC officer accessions and Air Force end-strength requirements, making OTS the most flexible source of new officers. Another unique feature is that the Air Force Recruiting Service (AFRS) recruits officer candidates who have already earned bachelor's degrees, which allows OTS to target specific Air Force academic degree needs.[2] Graduates must serve three years on active duty.

Direct Commission

This program commissions officers in the medical, legal, and religious fields. Typically, very few officers are commissioned this way. Those who do, join the Air Force after a brief (five-week) orientation course. Given the small numbers commissioned by this route and specialist nature of their skills, this program is not discussed further here.

This Report

Each year, roughly 3,000 cadets are commissioned as second lieutenant (O-1) line officers in the Air Force. All officers fall into one of two groups: line and nonline. Broadly speaking, *line officers* exercise command authority and lead the combat and combat support elements of the service. *Nonline officers* are specialists, such as doctors or chaplains. They do not command combat elements, although they can command units composed of specialists, e.g., a field hospital. This report focuses only on line officers. Line officers further divide into two groups: rated and nonrated. *Rated officers* fly regularly as part of their duties. These individuals hold such positions as pilots, combat systems officers (CSOs), air battle managers (ABMs), and pilots of remotely piloted aircraft (RPAs).[3] *Nonrated officers* are line officers who do not fly regularly as part of their duties but provide other specialties, such as maintenance and logistics.

The number of officers accessed each fiscal year (FY) must be regulated as one means of keeping the Air Force officer end strength at programmed levels. Additionally, accessions are spread across career fields to meet Air Force execution-year requirements. The classification process, which occurs near the end of an annual accession cycle, matches the cadets to career fields given their educational backgrounds; academic performance, including standardized aptitude scores and grade point averages; military and leadership skills; and career-field preferences. After the cadets enter active duty, they attend initial skills and pipeline training in their assigned career fields.

---

[2] AFRS's ability to recruit to specific degree requirements is influenced by some factors outside the Air Force's control, such as the economy.

[3] Within these categories, other distinctions frequently occur, such as pilot, senior pilot, and command pilot, which indicate increasing levels of skill and experience.

The goal of the Air Force officer accession process is to ensure the Air Force obtains and classifies officers qualified to perform various Air Force missions in particular career fields. Project sponsors in SAF/AQ and AF/A1P asked us to investigate, document, and assess current processes for obtaining line officer accessions with appropriate degrees, identifying any gaps between what the Air Force wants to achieve with its accession processes and recommending needed improvements to these processes.[4]

How We Went About the Study

Our approach to the study had four components. One was to evaluate the academic degrees necessary to staff the Air Force's career fields. The second was to analyze the overall Air Force officer accession process for meeting these needs, with a particular focus on matching AFROTC scholarship awards with accession requirements. To accomplish these goals, we conducted semistructured interviews with officer accession process owners and with career field managers (CFMs) responsible for identifying what academic degrees are important to their career fields. We also applied more broadly the survey work we began in FY 2013 to identify the required capabilities for officers in a career field and the mode of learning that best prepares the officer for each capability. We helped several CFMs apply what they learned from these surveys to define or refine their stated education requirements for accessions. Third, we analyzed the policies and practices for stating education requirements and then filling them with officers with the appropriate degrees and developed a new framework defining requirements, a new model for determining aggregate accession needs by degree type, and a method for evaluating whether education goals for accessions are being met. Finally, we collected, evaluated, and analyzed data on the use of AFROTC scholarships to meet officer accession requirements by degree.

How This Report Is Organized

The remainder of this report contains six sections. Section 2 summarizes the current line officer accession process, including the major participants in the process and the inputs and outputs each participant produces and uses. The remaining sections each present one of the major conclusions of our research, stated as a problem the Air Force must address, and each ends with our recommendations about what the Air Force should do to address it. The conclusions are stated in the subsection titles. Section 3 discusses the overall philosophy of what it means to establish and meet education requirements as defined by the career fields. Section 4 reviews the results of the FY 2014 classification of new accessions and proposes a feedback mechanism to

---

[4] We do not address commissioning processes for officers in other competitive categories, including Judge Advocate, Medical Corps, Dental Corps, Chaplain, Medical Service Corps, Biomedical Sciences Corps, and Nurse Corps.

score accession classification results each FY. Section 5 discusses the ways career fields might approach providing evidence or justification for requiring particular academic degrees. Section 6 proposes a method for improving the specificity of documenting academic degree requirements and discusses the implications of doing so. Section 7 investigates the application of AFROTC scholarships for meeting career field education requirements. Appendix A provides the details of the model we propose for determining education requirements by degree type. Appendix B lists the data on AFROTC scholarships we requested and what we received.

2. The Line Officer Accession Process

Overview

The officer accession process involves numerous offices and levels of involvement within the AF/A1 Manpower, Personnel, and Services community, as well as the Air Force Personnel Center (AFPC), Air Education and Training Command (AETC), and sources of commission (SOCs). With such a large number of participants, coordination and communication are important to the timeliness of this process. Table 2.1 lists the participants who determine the accession requirements. Figure 2.1 portrays the flow of the line officer accession process. The remainder of this section describes how the participants interact with each other and how each participant's output is used in determining the overall accession requirement.

Table 2.1. Participants in Determining Accession Requirements

Organization	Responsible Office	Office Symbol	Accession Requirement Contribution
Deputy Chief of Staff Operations	Force Integration Division	AF/A3OI	Requirements for production of rated officers
Deputy Chief of Staff for Manpower, Personnel and Services	Military Force Policy Division, Rated Issues	AF/A1PPR	Requirements for accession of rated officers
	Program Development Division	AF/A1MP	Aggregate (across all career fields) funded officer end-strength requirement, by Air Force specialty code (AFSC) and grade through the Future Years Defense Program (FYDP)
	Requirements Division	AF/A1MR	Aggregate (across all career fields) funded
	Force Management Division	AF/A1PF	Rated and nonrated accession requirements (specifically sustainment and dynamic targets)
	Accession and Training Management Division	AF/A1PT	Training accession requirements and classification requirements
U.S. Air Force Academy	Directorate of Strategic Plan and Programs, Requirements, Assessments and Analyses	USAFA/A5/8/9	Monthly projections of cadet strength and annual expected number of graduates

Figure 2.1. Line Officer Accession Process

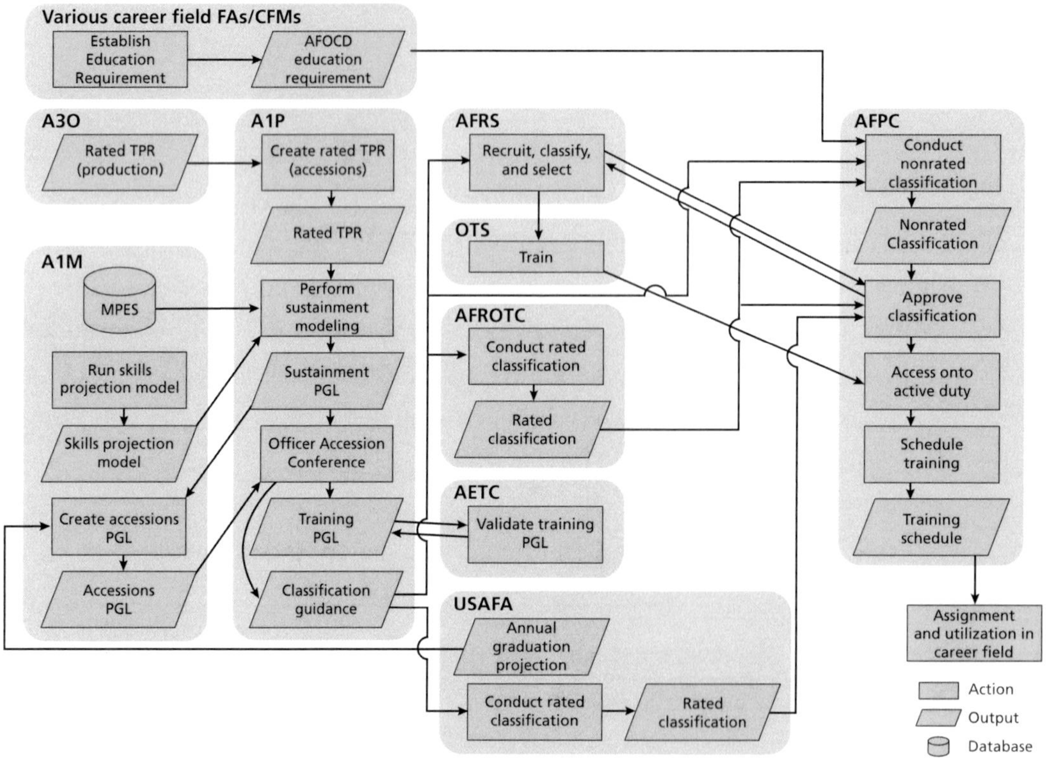

NOTE: MPES = Manpower Programming and Execution System.

Determining Accession Requirements

Broadly speaking, the accession process first determines the accession requirement for rated officers and then the requirement for nonrated officers.

Rated Accessions

The process starts with production of the rated trained personnel requirement (TPR) (top left of Figure 2.1, in the A3O block).[1] The first step in creating a rated TPR is to determine the number of requirements for production of rated officers across the FYDP. AF/A3OI determines total rated production requirements by identifying future empty rated positions by weapon system, taking into account undergraduate training availability. As the rated production requirement is the number of officers needed to fill future empty cockpits, the production is the number of officers who must successfully complete rated training. Once AF/A1PPR receives the

[1] For the purposes of this discussion, *rated* includes pilots, CSOs ABMs, and RPA pilots.

rated production requirement across the FYDP, it determines how many accessions are needed by applying aggregate attrition rates to account for the high number of washouts in the various rated training courses. The total rated accession requirement is the total rated production requirement plus an aggregate attrition factor. For example, if the attrition rate were 18 percent, the production requirement would be increased by 18 percent to ensure that the right number of rated personnel would be produced. Each SOC is assigned its share of the total rated accession requirement. Lastly, AF/A1PPR sends the accessions by FYDP required to produce the rated TPR to AF/A1PF for validation (A1P column in Figure 2.1).

Nonrated Accessions

AF/A1PF uses a steady-state inventory projection model to produce the sustainment program guidance letter (PGL) by three-digit AFSC, which includes both rated and nonrated requirements (fourth block down in the A1P column in Figure 2.1). AF/A1PF factors in the total number of rated accession requirements for pilots, CSOs, ABMs, and RPA pilots from AF/A1PPR, as well as the aggregate funded officer end strength, provided by AF/A1MR. These inputs allow AF/A1PF to determine the nonrated accession requirements by AFSC such that, when combined with the number of rated accessions, aggregate funded end strength and AFSC strength are maintained. The model produces two types of targets: a sustainment accession target, what each career field ideally needs to build and maintain its inventory to meet Air Force requirements, and a dynamic accession target, which is an execution-year target that incorporates end strength, the previous year's accessions, and an acceptable level of risk toward future career field health in terms of under- or overmanning.[2] AF/A1MP is involved in accessions through total officer strength management. AF/A1MP produces the accessions PGL, which specifies the total number of rated and nonrated officer accessions allocated to USAFA and the Holm Center (irrespective of career field).[3]

Officer Accession Conference

AF/A1PT uses both the accessions PGL and the dynamic targets from the sustainment PGL as a starting point for the officer accession conference (OAC), which occurs annually in fall. The goal of the OAC is to produce both the training accessions PGL and the nonrated line AFPC classification guidance. The training accessions PGL breaks down the dynamic targets provided

---

[2] In career fields that have seen recent shortages, the dynamic target could be higher than the sustainment target to make up for shortages; conversely, career fields that have seen accession overages in previous years may have dynamic targets lower than sustainment. Long-term impacts of under- and overaccessing in any one particular AFSC should, however, be carefully studied because of the promotion and force-shaping implications.

[3] The Holm Center provides coordinated leadership and policy direction for the Air Force's officer recruiting, training, and commissioning programs at Officer Training School and at Air Force ROTC detachments (Jeanne M. Holm Center for Officer Accessions & Citizen Development, 2015).

at the three-digit AFSC level into the different training courses to produce a rough draft of the training accessions PGL. AETC then determines whether it can train to the dynamic requirements, based on seat availability and other factors.

Concurrent with the training accessions PGL, the nonrated line AFPC classification guidance is produced at the OAC (fifth block in the A1P column in Figure 2.1). The classification guidance aims to determine the classification target by AFSC. Each CFM and functional authority (FA) is involved at the OAC to allocate the classification targets. The classification guidance also divides the accession targets between USAFA and the Holm Center, based on the aggregate totals provided in the accessions PGL and collaborative discussions between the USAFA and Holm Center representatives at the OAC. Both the training accessions PGL and classification guidance are produced at the OAC before confirmation of training levels from AETC. Thus, if AETC does not confirm the training capacities determined at the OAC and specifies different capacities, AF/A1PT must modify both the training accessions PGL and the classification guidance.

Classification

USAFA has three roles in the officer accession process: First, it provides annual graduation projections to AF/A1M to aid in producing the accessions PGL; second, it participates in the OAC to split the USAFA nonrated aggregate accessions among AFSCs; and third, it classifies USAFA cadets into rated career fields. The rated classification process occurs before the nonrated classification process and is done by the USAFA Cadet Personnel Office (USAFA/A1A). For cadets who prefer a rated AFSC (pilot, CSO, ABM, or RPA), a sufficiently high board order-of-merit score will likely guarantee selection into the rated AFSC; roughly 50 percent of USAFA graduates are classified into rated career fields (see the USAFA and AFROTC blocks in Figure 2.1).

The Holm Center is represented at the OAC by the AFROTC Deputy Registrar and by the Chief of Officer Recruiting from AFRS on behalf of OTS. AFRS represents OTS because OTS applicants have already earned bachelor's degrees and have been recruited, in part, because of their degrees. Holm Center representatives work together to generate an initial draft for the division of Holm Center accessions between AFROTC and OTS. The Holm Center typically splits its accessions, drawing 80 percent from AFROTC and 20 percent from OTS. The majority of STEM accessions are allocated to AFROTC, while OTS is allocated mostly nontechnical nonrated slots. However, because of its ability to ramp up quickly and respond to demand, OTS is often used to recruit and fill targeted career-field accessions that would otherwise go unfilled in the execution year.

In FY 2012, AFPC started classifying both USAFA and AFROTC cadets in a combined classification model for nonrated line officer accession requirements. This model sought to integrate USAFA and AFROTC nonrated line classification into one standardized process that included additional metrics important to senior leaders in the corporate Air Force. The combined classification model addressed several deficiencies:

- addressing lack of corporate oversight into classification policy
- meeting the Air Force needs through desired degree requirements
- creating a more equitable quality (as measured by quartile) distribution across all AFSCs
- unifying differing classification priorities and processes within each SOC
- providing a better solution for all parties concerned.

Several senior leaders prioritized the following metrics during an officer accession summit in June 2012: maximizing the ability to meet desired degree requirements, as stated by the Air Force Officer Classification Directory (AFOCD); a more equitable quartile distribution of cadets; and maximizing cadet preference rating.[4] The combined optimization prototype (which then became the current combined classification model) was approved for use at the June 2012 summit as well. The optimization model addresses the deficiency in not considering desired degree requirements by factoring in degree qualifications for each cadet toward meeting desired degree requirements by AFSC. The mandatory and desired degree qualifications are determined by the education entry requirements stated in the AFOCD. The optimization model is designed to maximize desired degree matches between cadets and AFSCs, meet mandatory degree requirements, and maximize cadet preference simultaneously, thereby providing better matches for both the cadet and the Air Force writ large. The combined classification model and the implications of the education requirements as stated in the AFOCD are discussed in greater detail in Section 4, where we discuss FY 2014 nonrated line officer classification results.

The optimization model provides an initial solution,[5] which is then passed to the classification approval authority, AFPC/DPSIP. AFROTC conducts rated classification before nonrated classification in a separate process, much like USAFA. Last, AFPC's Research, Analysis, and Data Division runs a different optimization model that schedules training for all graduating cadets based on their initial classifications (USAFA, AFROTC, and OTS in both rated and nonrated career fields). This model attempts to minimize casual status, which is the time between entering active duty and starting training.

---

[4] Each commissioning source ranks its cadets from 1 to N using an order of merit. While USAFA and AFROTC have differing methodologies for calculating order of merit, the same kinds of criteria are generally considered: academic performance, standardized test scores, physical fitness, and military and leadership assessment. The quartile distribution for each commissioning source is a 25 percent, 25 percent, 25 percent, and 25 percent distribution by 1 to N order-of-merit ranking.

[5] The initial classification determines the core AFSC, which is the career field an officer starts his or her military career in and is linked to the initial training that the officer will attend. The core AFSC assigned is either a rated or a nonrated AFSC, and the officer will remain either rated or nonrated for his or her entire career. The common exception is an officer attriting from rated training, who will likely be reassigned to a nonrated career field through a reclassification process. An officer can switch career fields later, but this must be approved, which is not guaranteed and depends on other factors, such as manning, end strength, and force management. An officer who switches career field is required to meet the AFOCD education entry requirement for the new career field.

Through meetings with stakeholders, we found that coordination among them is good but imperfect, with the kind of disconnects that can be expected with a large number of players and diffuse accountability. The remaining sections highlight the disconnects and gaps we identified with respect to meeting accession education requirements and provide recommendations to address these gaps and improve the overall performance of the officer accession process.

3. An Overarching Education Requirement Philosophy Is Needed

The most serious gap in the current accession process that we uncovered is the lack of agreement on the role academic degrees should play in qualifying an individual for classification into a particular AFSC. The type of undergraduate academic degree an individual has earned has little bearing on acceptance to a rated career field. However, nonrated career fields establish education requirements for entry. The Air Force has established that these functional areas or career fields are responsible for providing the trained and ready personnel to perform and support various Air Force missions. The FA and CFM are in the best position to know which or whether particular types of bachelor's degrees are desired or mandatory for their career field (AFI 36-2640).

Of course, an undergraduate academic degree is not the only requirement for new officer accession. The SOCs are charged with ensuring their graduates meet various other standards, such as leadership, ethics, and physical fitness. All new officer accessions meet these "whole person" qualifications and have bachelor's degrees qualifying them to serve as Air Force officers. The accession process in general, and the classification process should specifically, then, attempt to meet the education requirements established by the career fields. The extent to which the Air Force attempts to meet the education requirements the career fields have established for their accessions can be illustrated on a spectrum, as depicted in Figure 3.1.

The figure presents three approaches: meet only the mandatory requirements, meet the mandatory requirements and distribute the remaining spaces to those who have a desired degree, and meet both the mandatory and desired degree requirements. The remainder of this section discusses the three approaches to meeting education requirements depicted in the figure.

Figure 3.1. Education Requirements Philosophy Spectrum

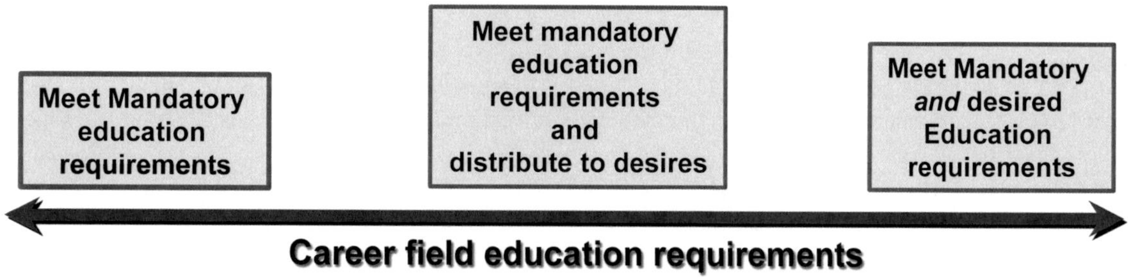

Meet Only Mandatory Education Requirements

The agreed-on philosophy could be to meet *only* the education requirements considered mandatory (on the left end of the spectrum in Figure 3.1). Currently, only six AFSCs have exclusively mandatory degree requirements, that is, everyone in each field must have a specific type of degree.[1] An example would be that an individual joining the 62E career field must have an engineering degree. Other career fields have mandatory degree requirements but do not restrict everyone entering the field to one type of degree. For example, some people entering the 38P career field must hold an operations research (OR) or an industrial engineering (IE) degree. Others must have a business degree, but other positions can be filled with individuals holding any degree.

Under this philosophy, the Air Force would focus recruiting efforts only on the mandatory degree requirements and emphasize other aspects of an individual's qualification when deciding if they should be admitted to USAFA or the AFROTC Professional Officer Course (POC).[2] In this case, it would be necessary to document only mandatory academic degree needs, since desirable academic degrees would be ignored in the selection processes. However, the knowledge and skills a new accession has acquired during an undergraduate academic degree program represent a valuable Air Force resource that should be capitalized on. This limited attempt to meet education requirements may not best serve the either career fields or the Air Force overall.[3]

Meet Mandatory Education Requirements and Distribute Desirable Degrees When Possible

Moving to the right on the spectrum in Figure 3.1, the philosophy could be to recruit to mandatory education requirements and distribute individuals with other types of degrees to career fields desiring particular degrees. Most career fields currently list mandatory or desired academic degrees in the AFOCD. In this case, success would be classifying an electrical

---

[1] The mandatory AFSCs are Civil Engineering (32EX), Developmental Engineering (62EX), Operations Research Analyst (61AX), Chemist/Nuclear Chemist (61CX), Physicist/Nuclear Engineer (61DX), and Weather (15WX). Some other AFSCs have a mandatory degree requirement for at least some portion of the career field, while some have only desired degree types.

[2] The AFROTC program consists of two phases, the General Military Course (GMC) in the freshman and sophomore years and the POC for juniors and seniors. The GMC is designed to improve communication skills and provide a window into military life. It is an opportunity for students to try out the program with no obligation (for those not on an AFROTC scholarship). Entry into the POC requires the individual to meet the requirements for active service and commit to at least four years of service after graduation.

[3] In previous research, we showed (Harrington, 2014) that this perspective can result in too few officers with STEM degrees for career fields with only partially mandatory STEM degree requirements, such as logistics, cyber, and space.

engineering graduate into 62E1E AFSC, those with human resources degrees being more likely to go to 38P AFSC than to other AFSCs, those with supply chain management degrees being more likely to go to 21R AFSC, and similarly for other AFSCs with nonmandatory academic degree requirements.

Under this philosophy, the Air Force would still focus recruiting efforts only on mandatory degree requirements and would emphasize other aspects of an individual's qualification when deciding whether to admit the individual to USAFA or the AFROTC POC. In this case, it is necessary to document mandatory academic degree needs, but career fields would also continue to express the degrees they desire, although resources would not be expended to meet these desires.

With this philosophy for meeting education requirements, career fields are able to take advantage of individuals in the population with desirable skills. Still, career fields are not guaranteed to receive accessions with the academic degrees FAs and CFMs desire unless they can provide justification that their requirement is mandatory and recategorize it as such.

Meet Mandatory and Desired Education Requirements

On the far right side of the spectrum in Figure 3.1, the Air Force could structure processes to meet both mandatory and desired career field education requirements. This philosophy requires establishing aggregate accession requirements and then recruiting, managing, and classifying accessions to meet these targets. In this case, the goal for success would be providing for 62E1E's mandatory electrical engineering graduates and also for 38P's human resource management graduates, 21R's supply chain management graduates, and all the other desired degrees for various career fields. While the goal would be to meet all degree requirements, in execution, if they could not be met, mandatory career field requirements would be met first and then, to the extent possible, desired degree requirements.

This viewpoint orients the SOCs and the overall accession process toward producing high-quality leaders for the Air Force and, at the same time, providing appropriately educated graduates for duty in career fields. This philosophy requires career fields to establish and document their education requirements.

Differing Viewpoints Among Air Force Senior Leaders

Over the course of our research, we observed that senior leaders differ considerably in their views about which position on this spectrum is most appropriate. The AF/A1 community, while recognizing its responsibility to access qualified new officers, also recognizes the resources that must be expended to recruit and perhaps to provide cadets incentives to pursue hard-to-recruit degrees (such as STEM degrees). On the other hand, nonrated FAs who value technical skills have found that they must describe their education requirements as mandatory (even if the requirement is not truly needed for all accessions) to be able to compete for at least some accessions with the degrees and skills the career fields need. Some senior leaders have expressed concerns that diversity will suffer in the face of increasing technical degree requirements, while others argue that, no matter what academic degree individuals obtain, they are Air Force officers and thereby qualified to lead in all but the most technical fields.

As it stands today, the Air Force currently has established some of the necessary portions of the process to meet both mandatory and desired education requirements; however, the result is a system that is at the middle of the spectrum. While career fields currently establish both mandatory and desired academic degree requirements and there is an attempt to provide career fields with their mandatory desired degrees, there is no agreement on how much effort and resources should be expended to recruit and access to the desired degrees. Research and recommendations presented in this paper will help to move the Air Force toward better meeting career field needs and better establishing the resources to be expended in meeting required and desired degree types.

Recommendations

We recommend that the AF/A1, responsible for providing the human capital for Air Force missions, clearly state the Air Force philosophy for establishing education requirements for Air Force officers. This policy should be communicated across the Air Force—to FAs and CFMs who are responsible for setting education requirements and to organizations supplying new officer accessions, such as AETC and USAFA. In addition, AF/A1 must ensure that officer accession processes and targets as outlined in Section 2 align with the overarching philosophy.

4. Classification Results Should be Assessed and Reported to Meet Career Field Needs More Effectively

In September 2013, the new (or combined) classification model was used to execute the FY 2014 nonrated line officer classification, a process that assigns graduating cadets from USAFA and AFROTC to nonrated line officer career fields based on their earned undergraduate degrees, their stated career field preferences, and their order-of-merit ranking, as well as the nonrated line officer career field education requirements and the classification targets for each AFSC. Each commissioning source ranks its cadets from 1 to N using an order of merit. While USAFA and AFROTC have differing methodologies for calculating order of merit, the same kinds of criteria are generally considered—academic performance, standardized test score, physical fitness, and military and leadership assessment—to arrive at a whole-person assessment. Before using the new classification model, USAFA and AFROTC nonrated line officer classifications were done separately, and each process used different characteristics with varying degrees of importance to inform the classification results.[1] The new model took advantage of several efficiencies: streamlining the characteristics used to inform classification decisions while providing career fields with higher numbers of cadets who match career field education requirements, more cadets receiving the career field assignments they prefer, and career fields receiving a more equitable share of lower-quartile cadets.

While the new model addressed several concerns surrounding the classification subprocess, our assessment of officer accession processes identified a missing analysis and the need for a communication feedback loop linking the nonrated line officer classification results by career field to the education requirements AFOCD specifies for each career field. AFPC did perform a classification analysis to make sure that every cadet received an assignment and that each career field received the appropriate number of cadets. AFPC also presented the aggregate result for each important metric (maximizing desired degree match, more-equitable quartile distribution, and maximizing cadet preference). However, we contend that an AFSC-by-AFSC analysis from the viewpoint of the AFOCD education requirements analysis is missing. Thus, in response to our sponsors' request, we performed an AFSC-by-AFSC FY 2014 classification analysis from the viewpoint of the education entry requirements as stated in the April 2013 AFOCD.[2] No

---

[1] Armacost and Lowe, 2003, discusses the optimization model used to classify USAFA cadets until FY 2013; AFPC used a model based on Armacost and Lowe's model to classify AFROTC cadets until FY 2013.

[2] The April version of the AFOCD within the calendar year that classification is performed is the version used for informing the accession education requirements because this is the version of the AFOCD cadets use when stating their career field preferences and determining degree qualifications (HQ AFPC, 2013).

nonrated line officer classification analysis had previously been conducted from this vantage point, and the results were illuminating.

The remainder of this section describes the analysis showcasing several career fields as examples and provides a standardized layout for observations and concerns at both the strategic and tactical levels, based on each AFSC's result. The examples are presented in a report card format that shows how well the classification results matched each career field's education requirements while showing what each career field received compared with the aggregate classification results. Last, we provide some recommendations and tie these into the education requirement philosophy discussion presented in the last section.

Assessing Classification Model Goals

The new classification model simultaneously maximizes meeting desired education requirements and cadet preference while not exceeding upper bound constraints on third and fourth-quartile cadet assignments for certain AFSCs, meeting AFSC targets for number of cadets assigned to each AFSC, and meeting mandatory education requirements if they exist for that AFSC.[3] As discussed earlier, AFSCs in AFOCD can either state mandatory education requirements (such as the engineering and scientist career fields) or desired education requirements (the majority of nonrated line officer career fields). So each undergraduate degree earned by a cadet either satisfies a mandatory education requirement, satisfies a desired education requirement, or is not considered a qualified degree for each career field. The desired degree match is then the percentage of cadets assigned to AFSCs that meet either the mandatory or desired education requirement for the AFSCs. Cadet preference, as shown in the classification analysis, is the percentage of cadets assigned to that career field that had listed that career field as one of their top three choices.[4] The third- and fourth-quartile upper bounds are to ensure that large career fields (classification guidance target greater than or equal to 30) do not receive a disproportionate amount of third- and fourth-quartile cadets. The metrics senior leaders deemed important, on which the success of classification is supposed to be based, are the following in order of priority:

1. maximizing the match rate of desired education requirements
2. satisfying the third- and fourth-quartile constraints
3. maximizing cadet preference.

[3] The quartile distribution for each commissioning source is a 25/25/25/25 percent distribution of the commissioning source's 1 to N order-of-merit ranking, which include cadets assigned to both rated and nonrated career fields. Note that the remaining quartile distribution once cadets assigned to rated career fields are removed is no longer a 25/25/25/25 percent distribution.

[4] Cadets may list up to six valid career field choices in order of preference, with choice 1 being the career field most preferred, but the consensus is that receiving choices 4–6 is not really receiving a preferred assignment.

Thus, for each AFSC, we report the FY 2014 classification results in terms of these three metrics and of any observations or concerns we noticed about how education requirements (as defined in the April 2013 version of AFOCD) affect the actual composition of cadets who are assigned to that career field. For metric 1, we present the percentage of undergraduate degrees earned by cadets assigned to each AFSC that meet either a mandatory or desired education requirement in accordance with the April 2013 version of the AFOCD. We also present the percentage of cadets assigned to the career field that have STEM degrees because two career fields state a minimum percentage of assigned cadets with STEM degrees and because the Air Force is interested in tracking STEM-degreed accessions. For metric 2, we present the percentages of cadets assigned to each career field by each quartile, and for metric 3, we present the percentages of cadets who listed a career field as a top-three choice and were assigned to that career field. We present three AFSCs as examples of how the analysis was conducted: Developmental Engineers (62E) as an example of a career field with mandatory education requirements, Personnel (38P) as an example of a career field with some mandatory education requirements, and Logistics Readiness (21R) as an example of a career field with no mandatory education requirements (desired education requirements only). The grading protocol is roughly as follows

- **A** if all mandatory or partial mandatory requirements were met **and** the career field received a desired degree match percentage that is close to or above the average **and** the career field received percentages of third- and fourth-quartile cadets similar to what existed in the nonrated cadet pool **and** the percentage of cadets assigned to the career field and listed the career field as one of their top-three choices is close to or above the average (see Developmental Engineers [62E] grade)
- **B** if all mandatory or partial mandatory requirements were met **and** one of the following clauses is true: the career field received a desired degree match percentage that is below the average **or** the career field received percentages of third- and fourth-quartile cadets in excess of what existed in the nonrated cadet pool **or** the percentage of cadets assigned to the career field and listed the career field as one of their top-three choices is below the average
- **C** if two of the **or** clauses in the B grade are true (see Logistics Readiness [21R] grade)
- **D** if three of the **or** clauses in the B grade are true
- **F** if no mandatory or partial mandatory requirements were met (see Personnel [38P] grade).

Example AFSC 1: Developmental Engineers (62EX)

In accordance with the April 2013 version of the AFOCD, developmental engineers lists the following mandatory education requirements: undergraduate engineering degree in the specialization identified by the suffix Aeronautical (A), Astronautical (B), Computer (C), Electrical (E), Mechanical (H), or General engineer (G). Each suffix denotes an engineering shred (i.e., allocation); to qualify for an engineering shred, a cadet must have a degree that matches the suffix, e.g., an electrical engineering degree qualifies an individual for the electrical engineering shred (62EXE). To qualify for the general engineering shred, the cadet must have earned an engineering degree. Given this mandatory education requirement and the fact that all classification results from the model must satisfy the constraints to meet mandatory education requirements, it is not surprising to see that developmental engineers received 100-percent degree match (see Figure 4.1, top table, column 3) for its 100-percent mandatory education requirement at both the career field level and for each specialization or shred (see Figure 4.1, top table, column 2). Also, because all engineering degrees are STEM degrees, there was a 100-percent STEM degree match as well. Figure 4.1, top table, column 4 shows the percentages for degree match and STEM in the aggregate (all cadets assigned to all AFSCs). The middle table shows the quartile distribution of cadets assigned to developmental engineers as compared to the aggregate quartile distribution of all cadets needing an assignment.[5] The bottom table shows the

Figure 4.1. Report Card for FY 2014 Developmental Engineer (62E) Nonrated Line Officer Classification Result

Developmental Engineer (62E)

Grade: A

Desired/Mandatory Degree Type			
Criterion	**AFOCD Mandatory Req (%)**	**% 62E Meeting Mandatory**	**All Accessions**
Degree Match	100%	100%	74%
STEM	100%	100%	42%

Quality/Quartile Spread				
AFSC	**Q1**	**Q2**	**Q3**	**Q4**
62E	32%	25%	25%	18%
All Accessions	20%	24%	26%	30%

Cadet Preference	
% Receiving 1 of Top 3 Choices	
62E	93%
All Accessions	82%

---

[5] Note that the remaining quartile distribution once cadets assigned to rated career fields are removed is no longer a 25/25/25/25 percent distribution.

percentage of cadets assigned to developmental engineers that listed developmental engineers as one of their top-three choices against the aggregate percentage of cadets receiving one of their top-three choices. The classification result for developmental engineers received an A because all constraints were met (mandatory education requirements and third- and fourth-quartile constraints) and because the career field received a higher percentage of cadets who expressed a preference for this career field.

Example AFSC 2: Personnel (38PX)

The 38P career field modified its education requirement in the April 2013 version of the AFOCD to state the following:

> undergraduate academic specialization in finance or accounting, economics, public administration, or human resource management is desirable; undergraduate degree in operations analysis, operations research, industrial engineering, management engineering, or mathematics for 25 percent of 38P accessions is mandatory; undergraduate academic specialization in business administration for 25 percent of 38P accessions is mandatory.

Therefore, we would expect 25 percent of 38P accessions to have some undergraduate degree akin to OR and 25 percent of 38P accessions to have a business management degree. The remaining 50 percent can have any undergraduate degree, but the model's matching process will try to assign cadets who have earned a desired degrees listed above. We describe the 38P career field as having partial mandatory education requirements, meaning that there are mandatory education requirements but that not all accessions are required to meet the mandatory education requirements. So, we categorize any career field with more than a 0 percent and less than a 100 percent mandatory education requirement into a newly emerging group of AFSCs that have partial mandatory education requirements; as of the April 2013 version of the AFOCD, this new partial mandatory AFSC group contained Nuclear and Missile Operations (13N), Space Operations (13S), Cyberspace Operations (17D), and Personnel (38P).

The 38P FY 2014 classification results show that the partial mandatory constraints were not met (see Figure 4.2, top table, column 3, highlighted in red); after discussing the result with the 38P CFM and AFPC, it was determined that the definition of degrees used to meet the two 25-percent mandatory education requirements did not match the list of degrees the 38P CFM deemed acceptable (this was a failure of an accurate statement of requirements rather than an error in the formulation or performance of the classification model). For example, the 38P career field was assigned cadets who had earned economics degrees to meet the 25 percent OR requirement and cadets who had earned finance degrees to meet the 25 percent business administration requirement. This result highlighted the concern that the CFM's intent, as expressed by the accession education requirement, can differ from how AFPC interprets the accession education requirement statement.

The middle table compares the quartile distribution of cadets assigned to 38P with the aggregate quartile distribution of all cadets needing an assignment. The orange highlighted square in Figure 4.2 (middle table, column 4) shows that 38P received more than its fair share of third-quartile cadets. Because of how the 25-percent mandatory education requirements were implemented, 38P as a whole was not placed under the same constraint to limit the third- and fourth-quartile cadets, even though the aggregate target for 38P was large enough to warrant application of the constraint. This was an unintended consequence of a first-time implementation of partial mandatory constraints. However, without an AFSC-by-AFSC analysis, this unintended consequence would have remained hidden. This result suggests that the third- and fourth-quartile constraints should be applied to the aggregate assignment of cadets to 38P regardless of whether the cadets are meeting either of the 25-percent mandatory education constraints.

Figure 4.2. Report Card for FY 2014 Personnel (38P) Nonrated Line Officer Classification Result

Grade: F

Personnel (38P)

Desired/Mandatory Degree Type			
Criterion	**AFOCD Mandatory Req (%)**	**% 38P Meeting Mandatory**	**All Accessions**
Degree Match	25% Math/IE/OR 25% Bus Admin	7% 16%	74%
STEM	25%	21%	42%

Quality/Quartile Spread				
AFSC	**Q1**	**Q2**	**Q3**	**Q4**
38P	19%	27%	**31%**	23%
All Accessions	20%	24%	26%	30%

Cadet Preference	
	% Receiving 1 of Top 3 Choices
38P	78%
All Accessions	82%

NOTE: When counting the degrees earned by cadets assigned to the 38P career field, 41 percent of the cadets met a mandatory or desired degree requirement.

The bottom table of Figure 4.2 compares how many cadets assigned to 38P listed it as one of their top three choices with how many cadets in the aggregate received one of their top-three choices. The 38P field received slightly fewer preferred assignments than in the aggregate because of the number of cadets who best fit into the career field. A best-fit assignment occurs when the cadet has listed fewer than six valid career fields on his or her preference form and received an assignment that is not on his or her shorter preference list. The term *best fit* is used because a blank or invalid career field choice is interpreted to mean that the cadet would like the Air Force to place him or her where the Air Force has the greatest need. When a cadet lists six valid career field choices and is assigned a career field not on his or her preference list, we say the cadet has been "nonvolunteered" into this career field. The classification model's matching process is strongly weighted to minimize nonvolunteer assignments and moderately weighted to minimize best-fit assignments. With these definitions in mind, the 38P career field received a lower-than-average preference rating because of a number of best-fit assignments in an unsuccessful attempt to meet the partial mandatory education requirements.

Therefore, with these results in mind for the three metrics, the classification result for 38P received an F because the partial mandatory constraints were not met. This grade is meant to be provocative for two reasons: First, mandatory, even partial mandatory, means mandatory; thus on a pass-fail scale, this result is a failure for 38P. Second, the classification result highlights a sign of resistance toward a new way of thinking about accession education requirements. More-specific accession education requirements do not necessarily imply that career fields want more STEM graduates and do not imply wanting more higher-quality cadets (at the expense of other career fields). Rather, more-specific accession education requirements highlight that, in a time of personnel reductions, the career fields would like officers who are properly trained, for instance, to maximize return on investment (ROI) and work performance while potentially minimizing training. To be explicit, the model will meet all stated mandatory requirements; in this case, the 25-percent OR degree requirement was implemented in such a way as to allow cadets who did not have such degrees to satisfy the 25-percent OR degree requirement. So the model performed as it should based on the input data, but the result did not align with the career field's stated needs or desires in the AFOCD education requirement because of the incorrect interpretation of which degrees satisfied the AFOCD education requirement.

Example AFSC 3: Logistics Readiness (21RX)

In accordance with the April 2013 version of the AFOCD, the Logistics Readiness (21R) description lists the following education requirements as desirable: an undergraduate degree in logistics management, economics, management, business administration, computer science, information management systems, finance, accounting, petroleum engineering, chemical engineering, or industrial management. Given that this career field has a desired education requirement and is less related to more-traditional STEM career fields, we would not expect a 100-percent degree match, which Figure 4.3 (top table, column 3, highlighted in red) confirms.

However, the percentage degree match in this career field is significantly lower than the aggregate degree match and is the reason for the red highlighting. The middle table in Figure 4.3 shows that the 21R career field received more than its share of third- and fourth-quartile constraints, a side effect of the requirement for the accessions classification guidance target to be greater than or equal to 30 cadets for the third- and fourth-quartile constraints to apply. The population restriction was put in place to ensure that very small career fields with mandatory education requirements would receive cadets with the proper education, but 21R is an example of a career field disadvantaged by this rule. The bottom table in Figure 4.3 shows that the preference match for this career field was close to the aggregate rate. The classification result for 21R received a C because of its low desired degree match and a greater share of cadets from the bottom half of the quartile distribution. Both outcomes are likely side effects of the weight of cadet preference in the model.

Figure 4.3. Report Card for FY 2014 Logistics Readiness (21R) Nonrated Line Officer Classification Result

Grade: C

Logistics Readiness (21R)

Desired/Mandatory Degree Type			
Criterion	**AFOCD Mandatory Req (%)**	**% 21R Meeting Desired**	**All Accessions**
Degree Match	None	20%	74%
STEM	None	17%	42%

Quality/Quartile Spread				
AFSC	**Q1**	**Q2**	**Q3**	**Q4**
21R	14%	26%	**28%**	**32%**
All Accessions	20%	24%	26%	30%

Cadet Preference	
	% Receiving 1 of Top 3 Choices
21R	86%
All Accessions	82%

Additional Observations

While we presented three AFSCs that showcase mandatory, partial mandatory, and desired education requirements, we created a report card for each nonrated line officer AFSC. The following additional observations relate to the statement of accession education requirements in the April 2013 version of the AFOCD and the effect of the content of the education requirement on the types of cadets received in classification (from the AFSC perspective):

- Several career field descriptions list partial mandatory degree requirements but then state that, if the full degree requirement cannot be met, minimum credit-hour requirements in certain academic fields do need to be met. However, from the modeling perspective, this minimum credit-hour requirement negates the full degree requirement. From the modeling point of view, if the degree is mandatory, anything less would not completely satisfy the requirement. (In reality, minimum credit-hour requirements would partially satisfy the requirement in terms of the whole-person concept, which is better than not meeting a minimum credit-hour requirement). Minimum credit-hour requirements suggest that a full degree is not mandatory but something the career field simply desires and the mandatory requirement is actually the credit-hour requirement.
- Compounding the above issue is that credit hours for AFROTC cadets are self-reported in an online form asking for credit hours in broad categories that are not properly defined for the cadet and are not verified by an advisor who understands these broad categories. Therefore, AFPC is likely unable to verify credit-hour requirements, rendering the credit-hour requirement unusable.
- The education requirements for several career fields are written in such a way as to contain redundancy and actually hinder the career field from receiving cadets with more specialized degrees in favor of cadets having obtained more-general degrees. For example, 21A, 21M, and 21R fields all list logistics management as a desired degree but also list management as a desired degree. Because logistics management is a management degree, this statement is redundant. Moreover, because degrees listed are not prioritized, the logistics management degree is as desirable as any other management degree, thereby reducing the chances that a cadet who has earned a logistics management degree will be assigned to one of these fields.
- Airfield Operations (13M) lists the following accession education requirement as desirable: undergraduate academic specialization in a technical discipline with courses in administration and management. This requirement does not clearly convey the intent of the 13M CFM because its definition of "technical discipline" is ambiguous and because it does not specify the number of courses or credit hours in administration and management. Additionally, cadets are graduating with Aviation Management and Aviation/Flight Operations degrees and are not being assigned to 13M, even though the majority of these cadets listed a preference for 13M. In effect, AFPC's classification model does not recognize Aviation/Flight Operations as meeting the desired education requirement.

Not related to a particular AFSC, but a comparison of FY 2014 degree production by academic field with degrees requested by the career fields shows an overproduction of degrees in criminal justice and criminology, political science, foreign language and foreign area, and history. Only Security (31P) desires criminal justice and criminology degrees. Only Intelligence Officer (14N) desires political science, history, and foreign language or foreign area studies degrees. Yet neither career field desires solely these specific degrees, so more such degrees are produced than the two fields actually require. Section 7 offers further proof of this we look at AFROTC scholarship production by degree or academic field in relation to AFSC sustainment requirements.

Recommendations

The classification analysis independently reinforced the need for a new method of stating education requirements (such a method is described in Section 6). In addition, we recommend the following process improvements to rectify other issues mentioned in this section:

- Institute a feedback loop from AFPC to AF/A1 and CFMs during execution when mandatory or desired degrees cannot be met because of degree shortages in the graduating cadet pool.
- Institute a feedback loop from AF/A1 to AFROTC to facilitate alignment of POC selection and scholarship offerings to career field needs.
- Treat partial mandatory AFSC requirements as mandatory requirements.
- Apply the third- and fourth-quartile upper-bound constraints to the aggregate AFSC target for career fields with (multiple) partial mandatory constraints.
- Complete and disseminate an annual postclassification analysis to AF/A1, SOCs, and CFMs. The postclassification analysis should, at a minimum, include the kind of AFSC-by-AFSC analysis presented here in a report card format. It should also include a discussion of recent degree production trends and how well the degrees the cadet pool has earned align with the education requirements in the AFOCD and which career fields are not receiving cadets that match its stipulated education requirements. This kind of analysis would necessitate discussing with the SOCs ways to address the shortages, help CFMs have more realistic expectations, and help all involved parties better understand how this process works.

5. Career Fields Lack Evidence-Based Methods for Determining Education Requirements

Coupled with the lack of an overarching philosophy for meeting educational requirements, two additional gaps are evident in the officer accession process: an evidence-based method for establishing education requirements for entry into an AFSC and an adequate method for documenting these education requirements. This section describes our proposal for dealing with the first of these missing pieces.

An Evidence-Based Method for Establishing Education Requirements

Background and Motivation

In the 2012–2013 time frame, the Air Force had mandatory STEM-degree prerequisites for entry into four officer career fields. In addition, there was a perceived need for STEM-related competencies among a significant portion of officers in other functional areas, such as acquisition management, intelligence, and cyberspace. In most cases, however, mandatory and desired degree requirements were not based on strong evidence. Moreover, a process to measure and quantify the perceived need for officers with STEM degrees was lacking.

To address these shortcomings, SAF/AQ asked RAND Project AIR FORCE (PAF) to develop a process for estimating degree requirements. Specifically, PAF's role was to design an approach, refine it, and aid in its implementation. The approach was designed to be a tool for CFMs and their staffs to use to analyze their education requirements. The method was also designed to be used to refine education requirements over time as career field needs evolve because of changes in missions, organizations, position responsibilities, AFSC consolidations, etc. PAF sought to create an approach that provided rigor yet was feasible given the resources available to the CFMs. In FY 2013, three career fields—Acquisition Management (63A), Space Operations (13S), and Personnel (38P)—contributed to the development of this process. During 2013, they served as cases in the "pilot test" to provide feedback on the process itself and on the instructions drafted to guide CFMs and their staff in implementation. In FY 2014, Nuclear and Missile Operations (13N), Contracting (64P) and Airfield Operations (13M) participated as well.

Overview of Survey Approach

Our approach is depicted in Figure 5.1. It consists of five major steps and requires input not only from the CFM and his or her staff but also from officers currently assigned to jobs in the career field. While classic job-task analysis focuses on the full inventory of knowledge, skills, abilities, and other characteristics (KSAOs) an individual needs to succeed at a specific job, our

Figure 5.1. Overview of Process for Estimating Degree Requirements for Accessions

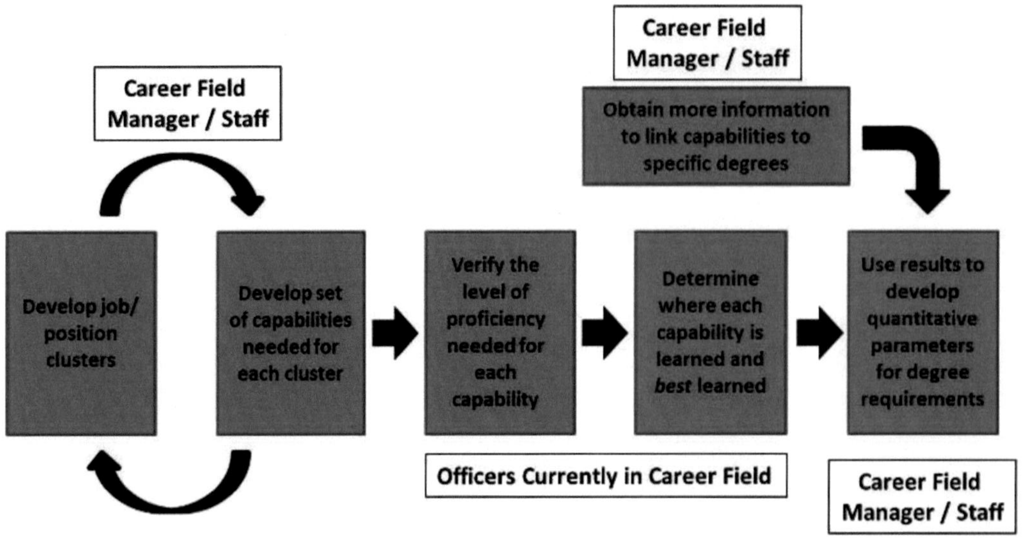

approach aims to reduce the level of effort required in two ways by: (1) focusing on "clusters" (i.e., groupings) of officer jobs or positions, instead of prescribing a position-by-position analysis, and (2) determining the set of capabilities an officer needs to succeed within a specific cluster, instead of assessing the full inventory of KSAOs.

According to this methodology, CFMs divide their career fields into distinct job clusters, identify the "capabilities" they believe officers need to perform their jobs within a specific cluster, and then survey officers in their career field to understand (1) the level of proficiency needed in each cluster and (2) where or how officers acquire the capabilities. Survey results, coupled with information about how different college degrees relate to different capabilities, are then used to inform changes to existing estimates of degree requirements. Capabilities needed at a higher level of proficiency and that are best obtained or acquired only through an undergraduate degree will be especially critical to capture in these estimates.

What Is a Job Cluster?

A *job cluster* is a grouping of jobs that are similar in terms of the work being performed, fall within the same duty area, or tend to represent a common career path for an officer. Alternatively, a cluster could be the same kind(s) of job but in different duty locations across the Air Force. In general, a job cluster can be viewed as a grouping of "like jobs," such as manpower staff or management engineering in 38P or operations crew, operations support, instructors/evaluators, and staff in 13S.

The purpose of developing job clusters is to arrive at a unit of analysis that is finer grained than focusing on an AFSC as a whole but not as resource intensive as a job-level unit of analysis. There is no one best way of determining job clusters for a career field; they should correspond to how career fields group officers while managing them across jobs. The *number* of clusters should be relatively small (fewer than six is strongly recommended), in part because the number of officers within each cluster should be large enough for statistically significant results (usually over 100 and for larger clusters over 500) and because each job cluster will entail a distinct data-collection effort (i.e., its own surveys). Ideally, these clusters will be mutually exclusive (i.e., officers fit into only one cluster), but if there is a lot of lateral movement or cross-functional work within a community, it may make more sense to allow jobs to fall within two clusters. Alternatively, creating a cross-functional cluster may be a solution.

What Is a Capability?

A *capability* is "a cluster of related knowledge, skills, and attitudes that affects a major part of one's job (a role or responsibility), that correlates with performance on the job, that can be measured against well-accepted standards, and that can be improved via training and development" (Parry, 1996, p. 50). A capability often is a synthesis or combination of KSAOs (or all four) to accomplish a specific job responsibility or mission. It may reflect not only possessing specific knowledge, skills, or abilities but also having the ability to apply them in a job-specific context. Capabilities generally focus on behaviors and abilities, but in some circumstances, deep-level knowledge or advanced skills could be considered a capability, particularly when it is a unique or critical characteristic. For the purpose of estimating degree requirements, the emphasis should fall on occupation-specific or unique capabilities for a job cluster.

Just as relying on job clusters is less resource intensive than analyzing all the jobs within a career field, so too is relying on capabilities rather than analyzing the full set of KSAOs that an officer needs to perform his or her duties in a specific job. In addition, the focus on a relatively small or narrow set of capabilities, rather than on an exhaustive list of everything an officer needs to know or be able to do to succeed, encourages CFMs to think carefully and critically about the most important qualities new officers must possess or quickly acquire.

For this approach, CFMs use their expert judgment and the expertise of their staffs to develop job-cluster specific capabilities. These are validated in the third step of the process (the third box in Figure 5.1, "Verify the level of proficiency needed for each capability"), in which job incumbents are asked to weigh in with their views of the capabilities.

For each job cluster, CFMs develop a list of the most important capabilities, such as mathematical reasoning, verbal communications. The emphasis should be on capabilities that are relatively specific to the job cluster (e.g., occupation specific), but not all have to be specific, especially if capabilities needed Air Force–wide are especially important for one of the job clusters.

Table 5.1 contains examples of capabilities for five career fields.

Table 5.1. Capabilities Examples from 2012–2013 Pilot Test Career Fields

Field	Capability	The Candidate . . .
Space, operations crew	Quantitative reasoning	Is able to synthesize data and work with incomplete data
	Weapon system knowledge	Is knowledgeable about the functionality, mission, and operation of a specific weapon system or set of weapon systems
	Communicate effectively	Conveys information and ideas; listens and responds to others
Space, instructors and evaluators	Training	Is able to help students learn the basics of systems they use; demonstrate proper use of checklists, documentation, etc.; run training classes; and explain complex systems and processes
	Mental agility, self-confidence, and tactfulness	Exhibits the mental agility, self-confidence, and tactfulness needed to manage and educate a group of students
	General space knowledge	Has the non–weapon-specific knowledge needed for instruction or evaluation
Personnel, manpower staff	Manpower data systems	Has a clear understanding of Air Force manpower data systems, including how they affect other Air Force data systems and business practices; demonstrates an awareness of which organizations use the data systems, as well as how and why
	Critical, analytical, logical thinking	Is able to think inductively and deductively, critically review documents, determine the root cause of a problem, identify connections between issues or phenomena, understand the implications of statutory or policy changes and other leadership decisions, and draw conclusions from limited or related information
	Stress tolerance	Is able to handle work pressure within an uncertain and variable environment, maintains poise even when subject to brusque treatment, and is effective in high-pressure situations with short-term deadlines and multiple top priorities
Personnel, management engineering	Continuous learning	Is willing to seek opportunities for continuous learning and thrives on the opportunity to explore new areas and delights in acquiring new knowledge about Air Force structure and missions, the determination of manpower requirements, and organizational principles
	Data synthesis	Is able to use different types of data, from multiple sources, to detect relationships and draw implications
	Modeling and simulation development	Is able to plan, create, evaluate, utilize, and obtain stakeholder endorsement for mathematical models, stochastic models, choice models, business process models, and simulations for application to Air Force manpower problems and is able to operate a range of modeling and simulation platforms
Acquisition management	Cost estimating	Has knowledge of policies and practices used in developing resource requirements and associated costs (e.g., funds, personnel, material, and facilities) for systems, structures, or facilities
	Writing	Recognizes and uses correct English grammar, punctuation, and spelling; communicates information (for example, facts, ideas, or messages) in a succinct and organized manner; produces written information, which may include technical material that is appropriate for the intended audience.

Table 5.1—Continued

Field	Capability	The Candidate . . .
	External awareness	Identifies and keeps up to date on key international policies and economic, political, and social trends that affect the organization; understands near-term and long-range plans; and determines how to best be positioned to achieve a competitive business advantage in a global economy

Gathering Evidence about Required Career Field Capabilities

The approach PAF developed in FY 2013 uses Adobe Acrobat and Microsoft Outlook to field the survey and initially process the responses. Survey respondents need to have only a computer, access to an email account, and Adobe Reader to complete and return the survey.

The process entails the use of two surveys. A CFM uses the Capabilities Survey to learn what the officers in a career field consider to be the level of proficiency necessary for each capability. Respondents rate each capability on a scale of 1 to 5, where 1 equals introductory level and 5 equals expert level.

The Modes Survey provides information about where or how the officers in the career field acquired each of the capabilities for their respective job cluster. Response options include the officer's bachelor's degree, a master's or graduate degree, training, normal duty assignments, professional military education, exercises, and outside the Air Force. Both surveys also include a short series of background questions, including a question in which the responding officer is asked to indicate the field of study in which he or she obtained a bachelor's and/or master's degree.

In an ideal world, feedback from a large number of officers in the Air Force would be collected to identify job-related capabilities and determine the optimal means for ensuring these capabilities are adequately represented in the workforce. However, surveys can be costly and require time from respondents, so we recommend balancing the resources expended for the survey with the desire for high-quality data by selecting an appropriate sample size.

Analyzing Survey Responses

These surveys can obtain significant information from officers serving in the field concerning the KSAOs they believe are necessary for success in the career field's mission and where these capabilities are obtained, and best obtained. Two analyses of survey respondent data are most directly tied to establishing education requirements: identifying where proficiency in important capabilities is best learned and examining variation in where capabilities are learned, by academic degree area.

Combining the capabilities and modes surveys, if respondents report that a capability an officer needs at an advanced proficiency is best learned or only learned through an undergraduate degree program, this analysis provides further evidence that an accession with a particular degree type is likely to be a primary way of meeting these workforce needs.

In the example depicted in Table 5.2, data collected on capability 2 suggest that accessions with appropriate undergraduate degrees may build workforce proficiency in this area. A high percentage of individuals in the cluster report a need for advanced or expert proficiency in capability 2, and the vast majority of survey respondents (89 percent) reported that the capability is best learned in a bachelor's program. The data for capability 3 look somewhat different. Despite a high percentage reporting that advanced or expert proficiency is needed, relatively few individuals reported that this capability was best learned by seeking a degree program.

To understand better the relationship between academic fields and capabilities, CFMs can analyze the data by simply calculating the percentage of survey respondents who reported that the capabilities are learned from a bachelor's degree program. In the example depicted in Table 5.3, nearly all the respondents with engineering or OR degrees indicated that the capability was learned in an undergraduate degree program. Relatively few respondents with history degrees reported this relationship, suggesting that the capability is more likely to be learned while obtaining an engineering or OR undergraduate degree than a history undergraduate degree. It is important to emphasize that the survey sample does not necessarily capture a representative population of degree holders, so many academic fields will not be represented.

Table 5.2. Example Data from Capabilities and Modes Surveys

	Reporting High Level of Proficiency Needed (%)	Those Who Learned Best Through Bachelor's (%)
Capability 2	76.2	89.4
Capability 3	64.2	22.2
Capability 4	48.3	58.5
Capability 1	22.1	74.5

Table 5.3. Example Data from Capabilities and Modes Survey, by Major Field

Academic Degree Type	Primary Relevant Learning Occurred in Undergraduate Work (%)
Business, management, marketing, and related support services	25.0
Engineering and OR	89.0
History	12.0
Mathematics and statistics	64.0
Other	32.0

Other Sources for Career Field Education Requirements

There are other sources and methods for obtaining evidence for career field education requirements besides the survey instruments described above. Some career fields may have certification requirements requiring a particular type of degree. For example, certain jobs in Civil Engineering (32E) require professional engineers, and the World Meteorological Organization requires particular types of degrees for Aviation Weather Forecasters (15W). These certifications can be the basis for establishing education requirements in career fields.

Some career fields have particular jobs requiring career-field-specific knowledge *and* technical knowledge, skills, or degrees. For example, some positions for nuclear officers at the Defense Threat Reduction Agency require knowledge of employment of nuclear weapons and the technical aspects of nuclear effects. Filling these types of jobs requires that at least some percentage of the career field have nuclear science or engineering degrees—a sufficient number of individuals to fill the positions but also additional individuals to allow people with the appropriate grade and experience to rotate through these positions. In addition, some career fields mirror academic degree programs. For example, the CFM for Financial Management (65F) may determine that there is a requirement for at least some portion of the field's new accessions to have accounting and finance degrees.

All career fields have unique aspects, so there may be various methods for establishing education requirements. What is to be avoided is establishing requirements based on uninformed perceptions about what a degree provides or on unsubstantiated opinions from career field senior leaders or CFMs that particular degrees provide the best foundation for success in a career field.

Recommendations

We recommend that AF/A1P establish a repository (perhaps the CFM SharePoint) for the survey templates and manual described here and that it encourage CFMs to administer these surveys to samples of their officers as their career fields change, as career fields are merged or split, or as the required KSAOs for job clusters change. We do not recommend mandating that the surveys be administered on a strict recurring schedule; as noted earlier, career fields are unique, and there may be significant considerations beyond survey results for establishing degree requirements. Still, it is important that A1P establish a process for validating or revalidating education requirements periodically to avoid expending unnecessary resources in recruiting and accessing hard-to-get academic degree types.

As more career fields implement the survey tool and as more response data become available over time, we would also recommend a review of the efficacy of the survey instrument and follow-on efforts to more closely tie the survey responses to academic degree needs.

6. Career Fields Lack an Effective Framework for Documenting Education Requirements

Once a career field gathers evidence for its officer education requirements, it must document the requirements in a way that ensures the officer accession process responds to this statement of need and provides accessions with the needed academic degrees. The authoritative source for this documented education requirement is currently a paragraph for each officer AFSC listed in the AFOCD. For example, the education requirement for the Acquisition Manager (63A) career field is as follows:

> Undergraduate academic specialization in engineering, engineering science, engineering management, mathematics, analytical science, physical science, business, or management; or completion of a minimum of 24 semester credit hours of study from an accredited institution of higher education from among the disciplines of: accounting, business finance, law, contracts, purchasing, economics, industrial management, marketing, quantitative methods, and organization and management is mandatory.[1]

This statement has several uses. USAFA and AFROTC cadets use this information to determine whether they are qualified for entry into an AFSC; AFPC uses this information in the accession classification model; and AF/A1P and the SOCs *should* use this information to influence degrees earned for future accessions. However, there are several problems with specifying education requirements in this current paragraph form:

- It does not prioritize the degrees listed.
- It does not specify the quantity of each type of degree desired.
- Degree titles may be too general to designate the specific academic degree required, and a mixture of specific and general degree types may be listed.
- Cadets self-report the number of semester hours they have in broad academic areas; there is no way to validate that cadets meet a credit-hour requirement.[2]

These problems with documenting degree requirements have consequences for the officer accession process:

- Because of the vagueness of the current statement of degrees required for entry into particular AFSCs, it may not be clear to USAFA and AFROTC cadets which AFSCs they qualify for.

---

[1] HQ AFPC, 2013.

[2] We have recommended to AF/A1PT how it might approach collecting this information and using it in the classification model. The organization is weighing the benefits of collecting this information for all cadets with the added resources it would take to ensure that the information is correct.

- The education requirements in paragraph form are not sufficiently specific for AFPC to know how to code the requirements in the classification model.
- The education requirement paragraphs lack sufficient information for AF/A1PT to sum across the requirements to establish accession targets by academic degree.

Improved Method for Communicating Career Field Needs

We recommend a new framework for documenting these education requirements that addresses these issues. Table 6.1 illustrates the new framework for the Acquisition Manager (63A) career field. The first column shows the prioritized tier with the most important degree requirements listed first. The second column lists the target percentage rate indicating the percentage of accessions belonging to that tier. This percentage can be specified as greater than, less than, or equal to, depending on the degree needs. The percentages do not need to sum to 100 percent; however, any total percentage less than 100 indicates that accessions with any academic degree are permitted.

The third and fourth columns show the allowable degree(s) in the tier specified according to the Classification of Instructional Program (CIP) code and the CIP degree titles. The CIP code provides a taxonomic scheme that supports the accurate tracking of and reporting on fields of study. The CIP was developed by the U.S. Department of Education and is a universally accepted way of communicating academic disciplines. The Air Force is currently transitioning to this format for degrees. CIP codes allow generalization at the 2-, 4-, or 6-digit degree code.

Table 6.1. Acquisition Manager (63A) Education Matrix

63A - *Acquisition Manager*

Tier	*Target Accession Rate*	*CIP*	*Education Program Description*	*Requirement*
1	> 50%	14.XXXX	Engineering	Mandatory
			or	
		40.XXXX	Physical Sciences	
2	> 30%	11.XXXX	Computer and Information Sciences and Support Services	Desired
			or	
		26.XXXX	Biological and Biomedical Sciences	
			or	
		27.XXXX	Mathematics and Statistics	
			or	
		52.XXXX (Excluding 52.04XX)	Business, Management, Marketing, and Related Support Services	
3	< 10%	15.XXXX	Engineering Technologies and Engineering-Related Fields	Permitted
			or	
		41.XXXX	Science Technologies/Technicians	

The fifth column designates the tier as mandatory, desired, or permitted. These terms are defined as follows:

- A **mandatory** degree is one that the career field must have to ensure a capability is obtained to meet mission requirements.
- A **desired** degree is one that the career field believes contributes to the capabilities officers in the career field need to execute their specified mission. A career field listing desired degrees will receive a lower priority than a career field listing the same degrees as mandatory.
- When all higher tiers have been met to the degree possible with individuals available in the accession cohort, **permitted** degrees become acceptable for the career field. Setting a less than or equal percentage means a career field will only take so many of these permitted degrees. If all tiers have been met to the degree possible and if the tiers do not sum to 100 percent, the career field is signaling that it would rather go short than take any more than the permitted percentage.

In Table 6.1, the top priority for the Acquisition Manager (63A) AFSC is mandatory: At least 50 percent of the accessions are to have some type of engineering or physical science degree. The next most important goal is a desire: At least 30 percent of the accessions should have a computer information or science, biology, math, or business management degree. By placing all these degrees together in tier 2, the career field is indicating that these types of degrees are equally acceptable. Since tiers 1 and 2 are "greater than" tiers, the career field would accept 100 percent of its accessions from these tiers. If that cannot be accomplished with the individuals in the accession cohort and with the individuals classified to other AFSCs, the 63A career field will permit no more than 10 percent of its accessions to have engineering, science, or technology degrees. Since tiers 1, 2, and 3 do not sum to 100 percent, the career field is saying that it would rather be allocated fewer total accessions than the number needed for sustainment if it means that these accessions will have degrees other than those listed in the education matrix.

Formatting education requirements in this way addresses many of the concerns, issues and observations noted during the assessment of classification results in Section 4:

- The matrix specifies percentages by tier, which provides clear targets.
- Although the percentages actually classified into career fields depend on the composition of the graduating cadet pool, the matrix clearly defines the career field's needs and priorities.
- The education requirement matrix allows prioritization of degrees, providing career fields the ability to prioritize specialized degrees over general degrees. For example, tier 1 could contain industrial management degrees, and tier 2 could contain management degrees, providing the Logistics Management (21R) career field greater opportunity to receive accessions with logistics management degrees.
- The education requirement matrix uses CIP codes to specify that degrees are mandatory, desired, or permitted, providing a clear definition of which degrees the CFM considers to be mandatory, desired, or permitted. AFPC can use can use the tiers and percentages in its classification model without interpretation or translation from AFPC analysts.

- The education requirement matrix emphasizes full degrees to meet requirements; this avoids concerns about determining credit hours. (AFPC is often unable to verify proper courses for credit hour requirements.)

Draft Education Matrices for Nonrated Line Career Fields

Using the education requirements paragraphs in the AFOCD, we constructed an education matrix for each nonrated line officer career field. As of the end of FY 2014, career fields were in the process of analyzing or updating their education requirements and developing their initial education matrices. Therefore, the matrices we developed are considered drafts and have not been approved by career field functional authorities. However, the method we show here can easily be updated as education matrices are adjusted over time.

With these draft matrices, we were able to sum across the career fields and identify the "high utility" degrees—those that the greatest number of AFSCs find desirable. Figure 6.1 shows these degrees and a list of the degrees most desired when the accession AFSCs are weighted by the average annual number of accessions. The education requirements currently stated in the AFOCD indicate that career fields, in general, most desire engineering, OR, mathematics, and physical science degrees. While aggregating education matrices in this way can inform degree targets, it may be that quantity is not the most important consideration and that it is very important to have a small number of highly specialized degrees. Individual career field priorities must remain visible in any setting of aggregate academic degree targets.

Figure 6.1. Aggregating Education Matrices to Identify High-Utility Degrees

Degree Group - Rank Ordered by Number of Career Fields
Electrical, Electronics and Communications Engineering
Mechanical Engineering Industrial Engineering
Aerospace, Aeronautical and Astronautical Engineering Architectural Engineering Chemical Engineering Civil Engineering Computer Engineering Environmental/Environmental Health Engineering Nuclear Engineering Petroleum Engineering
Various Types of Engineering Operations Research
Computational Mathematics Physics Chemistry Econometrics/Quantitative Economics
Computer and Information Sciences Mathematics
Business Administration and Management Operations Atmospheric Sciences and Meteorology
Social Psychology Management Science

Required, desired, accepted by more career fields ↓ **Required, desired, accepted by fewer career fields**

Degree Group - Weighted by Number of Career Field Accessions
Electrical and Electronics Engineering
Computer Engineering
Industrial Engineering
Computational Mathematics
Computer and Information Science
Chemical Engineering Petroleum Engineering Mechanical Engineering
Civil Engineering Environmental Engineering
Architectural Engineering Construction Engineering
Aerospace, Aeronautical, Astronautical Engineering Operations Research
Various Engineering Disciplines Mathematics
Various Physical Sciences
Management Science Business Administration and Management Research and Experimental Psychology
Economics Intelligence, Command, Control and Info Ops

Note:
- **Degrees grouped together in the lists above are of equal rank/weight**

Developing Accession Targets by Academic Degree Type

As described in Section 2, AFSC currently bases annual accession targets on the number required to sustain the AFSC, balanced by overall officer end strength. However, prior to the classification of graduating cadets, the SOCs should be working toward a required number of accessions by degree type. To date, no method for developing these degree targets (rather than AFSC targets) has been available because of the vague manner in which academic degree requirements are currently stated.

We developed a method that allows evaluation of whether an accession cohort meets the career field academic degree requirements and a method for establishing targets by academic degree type.

Let $x_{i,j,k}$ be the number of officer accessions for degree i in AFSC j and requirement tier k ($i = 1, \ldots, n$ degree types; $j = 1, \ldots, m$ AFSCs; $k = 1, \ldots, p$ possible tiers). Set $a_{j,k}$ as the minimum required number of accessions in AFSC j, tier k based on the information in each AFSC's education requirement matrix and the total number of accessions for each AFSC. The goal is to determine values for $x_{i,j,k}$ while meeting the required number of $a_{j,k}$ and while meeting the total number of accessions required in each AFSC. Constraints ensure that the solution differs as little from current practices as possible while still meeting each career field's requirements at each tier in the education matrix for each type of degree required. Appendix A gives the detailed notation for this optimization model.

With these variables and constraints, one may be tempted to attempt to solve for $x_{i,j,k}$ to determine exactly how many officers should be accessed in each degree type. However, because so many possible degree types can satisfy each AFSC and tier, a wide range of values for the variables $x_{i,j,k}$. would meet the constraints equally well. These constraints could, however, be used to test a particular group of accessions to see if it satisfies the degree requirements for each AFSC. The constraints could also be used to test whether a future or altered accession cohort with a different set of academic degrees will meet all career fields' education requirements.

At any time, the Air Force has officer candidates pursuing particular degree types in the pipeline at various stages in their academic programs. On graduation, the degrees many of these officer candidates have earned will satisfy many, if not all, of the education requirements the CFMs have defined. It may not be necessary to change radically the types of degrees accessed. Resources might be unnecessarily expended to recruit and access very different degree types; therefore, we could also search for a set of academic degrees that differs as little as possible from the current accession degree types but that still satisfies the requirements the CFMs have expressed in the education requirement matrices. One way to arrive at such a solution is to solve for $x_{i,j,k}$ given the constraints for the number of accession in each AFSC and tier and, at the same time, minimize the difference between the degrees career fields need and what the Air Force is currently accessing.

Rather than providing a single, definitive answer for the number of degrees that should be accessed in each year's accession cohort, we envision an iterative approach, with the model results informing academic degree targets and policy changes over time, as well as changes to the education matrices for individual career fields.

Model Results and Changes the Model Suggests

We used the model as described above to determine the academic degree targets that meet the draft career field education matrices we created and minimize the change from the FY 2014 pool of actual accessions for AFROTC and USAFA.[3] The FY 2014 pool of accessions did not meet the draft career field education matrix requirements; however, it took only a relatively slight shift in the number of degree types accessed to meet the requirements. Figure 6.2 shows the changes required to meet requirements, with positive numbers of accessions indicating the need to increase that type of degree and negative numbers indicating the need to decrease that type of degree. The scale along the bottom indicates one undergraduate degree of the type indicated.

Figure 6.2. Required Shift in Degree Types to Meet Career Field Education Requirements

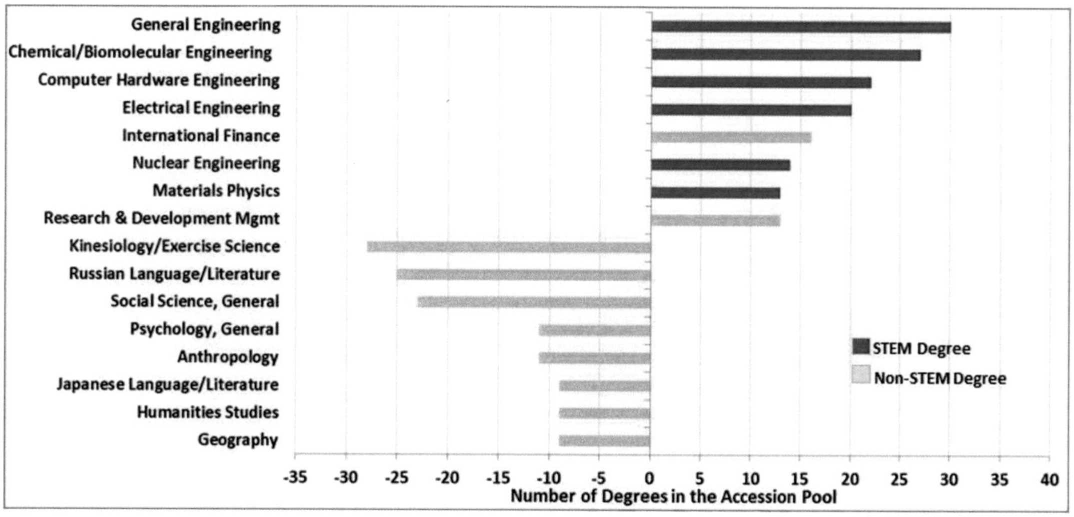

NOTE: This chart reflects only the largest positive or negative shifts. A total of 55 academic disciplines were analyzed, but many involved only one or two individual degrees.

---

[3] It is also possible to enter values in the model so as to minimize the change from an historical average of the actual accessions by degree type over some appropriate time frame. Doing so should dampen the impacts of the particular degrees in a single year's accession cohort.

In our analysis, 200 of 1,856 (11.2 percent) degrees were "swapped" in the solution from the set of current degree types to a new degree type. In general, agriculture, education, language, liberal studies, social science, and history degrees were exchanged for engineering, meteorology, research and development, management, and finance—from primarily non-STEM degrees to STEM degrees. The increases or decreases depicted minimize the change from the current average number of accession degrees. Degrees for which an increase is indicated were added to satisfy constraints for particular career field needs. Degrees for which a decrease is indicated either were not needed to satisfy career field needs or had too many degrees of that type in the accession pool.

It is also informative when developing aggregate accession goals to examine the model solution in terms of the minimum number of degrees by type in the solution needed to satisfy career field education matrix constraints. Table 6.2 shows the minimum number of degrees by type needed to satisfy career field requirements (continuing to use a solution as close to historic accession degrees as possible).

Table 6.2. Minimum Number of Degrees by Type Required to Meet Career Field Constraints

Academic Degree Type	Degrees Needed (no.)
Engineering	606
Business, management, marketing, and related support services	206
Physical sciences	131
Biological and biomedical sciences	128
Social sciences	100
Multi- and interdisciplinary studies	53
Homeland security, law enforcement, firefighting and related protective services	48
Computer and information sciences and support services	46
Mathematics and statistics	42
Legal professions and studies	27
Military technologies and applied sciences	19
Psychology	15
Transportation and materials moving	15
Engineering technologies and engineering-related fields	13
Natural resources and conservation	9
Public administration and social service professions	6
Architecture and related services	5
Communication, journalism, and related programs	3
Philosophy and religious studies	2
Visual and performing arts	2
Total	1,476

NOTE: Degrees grouped by two-digit CIP code.

Note that, of the 1,856 degrees in the solution, 1,476 (79.5 percent) are needed to satisfy career field degree requirements; the remaining 380 accessions could have any degree, and career field requirements would still be met. AF/A1PT can use this minimum set of required degrees to establish future accession targets for meeting career field requirements, while allowing flexibility for accessions with no specified degree required.

As mentioned previously, we cannot say that there is an "optimal" solution for several reasons:

- Other solutions certainly would satisfy the constraints. For example, rather than decreasing the number of officers with Japanese language degrees accessed, an equally acceptable solution might be to decrease the number of officers with Korean language degrees.
- The model uses as many current accession degrees as it can, even if they are filling lower tiers in education matrices that call for "any degree."
- Removing the requirement that the model solution be as close as possible to current accession degrees could result in a solution that is optimal in some other sense, for example, cost, adaptability, or as prerequisites for obtaining advanced degrees.

Recommendations

We recommend that AF/A1P mandate the format in Figure 6.1 as the standard for all nonrated career field education requirements. These education matrices can be used to accomplish the following:

- Clearly state priorities, desired percentages, mandatory/desired requirements and specific degree types for use in the classification model run by AFPC.
- Evaluate projected USAFA and AFROTC production with requirements stated in education matrices to determine potential gaps.
- Provide a clear representation of the qualifying academic degrees for the use of cadets listing preferences prior to classification.

We also recommend that AF/A1P compare projected accessions by academic degree type with aggregate career field requirements, as described in this chapter. Information obtained from reviewing the optimization model runs can be used to adjust the degree types that the SOCs produce and, over time, better meet career field degree requirements.

7. AFROTC Scholarship Production Is Not Aimed at Meeting Academic Degree Requirements

General Overview of AFROTC Scholarship Process

This section discusses an additional opportunity available to the Air Force to shape the types of degrees cadets earn through the AFROTC scholarship program. AFROTC is the largest commissioning source and is heavily relied on to commission officers who meet Air Force education accession requirements. Consistent degree production can, however, be difficult because AFROTC has 144 detachments that serve an even greater number of universities throughout the country, where cadets earn a degree of their choosing. However, the Air Force can influence the types of degrees AFROTC cadets earn by awarding AFROTC scholarships.

According to AFROTC Instruction 36-2011, AFROTC ensures the scholarship program targets students interested in pursuing degrees that correspond to Air Force requirements, recruits and retains students to meet officer production requirements, and provides an incentive to attract and retain the highest quality individuals. One overriding factor to keep in mind is the statutory requirement of 10 U.S. Code §2107 that requires 50 percent of AFROTC scholarships to be awarded to cadets and midshipmen who will attend college at the in-state tuition rate, which at times hampers AFROTC's ability to recruit potential cadets who would like to attend more prestigious universities or programs outside their of states of residence.

The Air Force relies on AFROTC to produce cadets with certain majors to fill hard-to-meet requirements, such as STEM, nursing, and foreign languages, and to attract exceptional officers regardless of major and officers who support diversity goals, which it does through its scholarship program. AFROTC has two main programs that offer college scholarships to cadets: the high school scholarship program (HSSP) and the in-college scholarship program (ICSP), which are awarded while the prospective cadet is in high school or college, as the names suggest. The operation of these programs directly affects the kinds of officers by degree type accessed.

High School Scholarship Program

AFROTC's twofold objective in the HSSP is to enable high school students to earn undergraduate degrees and simultaneously imprint the students with officership and leadership skills. Over 15,000 high school students apply to the HSSP every year, but roughly only 5,500 qualify and are interviewed and reviewed by a scholarship selection panel convened by Headquarters (HQ) AFROTC. The AFROTC scholarship selection boards determine an order of merit for each student, which allows AFROTC to rank and sort the students into the following categories: technical majors (a subset of STEM degrees to meet mandatory AFSC education requirements, such as engineering, science, and math), foreign language majors, nursing, and nontechnical majors. Students are offered the best scholarship available based on this ranking. Currently, AFROTC aims to offer 80 percent of the HSSP scholarships to students willing to pursue technical degrees and 10 percent to those willing to major in foreign languages. To attract exceptional students, AFROTC uses the remaining 10 percent to sponsor students pursuing nontechnical degrees. HSSP scholarships comprise about 50 percent of the annual scholarships.[1]

Several types of high school scholarships are used to attract students in different ways. Applicants awarded a four-year Type 1 scholarship can attend any AFROTC university at any cost. A Type 2 scholarship allows students to attend a school of their choosing and will pay up to $18,000 annually. A Type 7 scholarship must be used at an AFROTC university that the student can attend at the in-state tuition rate. Table 7.1 presents several types of four-year high school scholarships that AFROTC offers, the average annual cost, and number of cadets currently enrolled. Table 7.2 shows the acceptance rate for each scholarship type and category in FY 2011. AFROTC offered 969 scholarships to high school students and 612 were accepted. The breakdown is as follows: 77.4 percent of scholarships offered toward technical majors, 7.1 percent offered toward foreign language majors, and 15.5 percent offered toward nontechnical majors with an overall acceptance rate of 63.1 percent. The scholarship offer percentages are fairly close to their goal of 80 percent, 10 percent, and 10 percent, but they are limited by the order of merit and the cadets' willingness to enter into a contract to earn a technical or foreign language degree. Also, not surprisingly, students are more likely to accept the scholarship if the offer is more attractive, i.e., Type 1 or Type 2.

Table 7.1. AFROTC Scholarship Types, Costs, and Enrollment

Scholarship Type	Benefit Level	Average Annual Cost	Cadets (no.)	Percentage of Scholarships
1	Full tuition at any AFROTC school	$19,600	946	21
2	$18,000	$12,200	2,606	57
7	Full tuition at any AFROTC at in-state rate	$9,600	983	22

NOTES: The Air Force advertises three types of scholarships: 1, 2, and 7 (AFROTC, 2014). These provide the benefits listed above. However, the Air Force also offers versions of the three major types that provide somewhat lower benefits and are designated as types 3, 6 and 8 (Taylor, 2013). A type 1 scholarship pays full college tuition, most fees, and a book allowance. A type 2 scholarship pays college tuition, most fees up to $18,000, and a book allowance. If a student attends an institution where the tuition exceeds $18,000 per year, he or she pays the difference. A type 7 scholarship pays college tuition up to the equivalent of a public school's in-state rate and a book allowance. If a student receives a type 7 offer but wishes to attend a college or university for which he or she does not qualify under the guidelines, the student can convert the four-year type 7 scholarship to a three-year type 2 scholarship.

[1] Information provided by the deputy registrar of AFROTC/RR (Taylor, 2013).

Table 7.2. FY 2011 Scholarship Offers and Acceptances for Type 1, 2 and 7 Scholarships

Scholarship Category	Scholarship Type	Scholarships Offered (no.)	Scholarships Accepted (no.)	Acceptance (%)
Technical	1	103	73	70.9
Technical	2	242	176	72.7
Technical	7	405	218	53.8
Foreign language	1	1	0	0.0
Foreign language	2	22	17	77.3
Foreign language	7	46	22	47.8
Nontechnical	1	0	0	N/A
Nontechnical	2	103	89	86.4
Nontechnical	7	47	17	36.2

In-College Scholarship Program

The ICSP is much like the HSSP but awards scholarships to students who have already completed one year of college. Similar to the HSSP, AFROTC uses an algorithm to calculate orders of merit, which it uses to award scholarships. In-college scholarships within the ICSP are awarded through a nationally competitive process, by category, in the following priority based on order-of-merit ranking: critical technical degrees (meteorology, computer engineering, electrical engineering, nuclear engineering, and nuclear physics), technical degrees (engineering, science, and math), foreign languages, students at historically black colleges and universities; students at Hispanic-serving institutions; and nontechnical degrees. The ICSP awards two- and three-year scholarships that comprise the other roughly 50 percent of annual scholarships awarded.[2]

Professional Officer Course Selection

Roughly 6,000 freshmen and 5,000 sophomores participate in AFROTC, but only 2,000 to 2,500 undergraduates are chosen to go into the POC, which begins after the sophomore year. In general, the Air Force seeks to commission all POC graduates and aims to meet its production requirements by having 75 percent of cadets on scholarship following the POC selection process. To meet that requirement in FY 2013, AFROTC set the following objectives: 735 STEM majors, 115 foreign language majors, 60 nurses, and 590 high-quality cadets, for a total of 1,500

---

[2] Information provided by the deputy registrar of AFROTC/RR (Taylor, 2013).

scholarships out of the 2,000 total production goal. The aim was to seat 700 of these 1,500 through the HSSP and the remaining 800 through ICSP.

The POC lasts a minimum of four semesters, so cadets are contracted in the spring of their sophomore year. As with HSSP and ICSP, an order-of-merit score is calculated for all POC nominees. The order-of-merit algorithm used for selection process applies the following weights: 50 percent detachment commander ranking, 20 percent cumulative grade point average, 15 percent physical fitness aptitude, and 15 percent toward a Scholastic Aptitude Test–equivalent score. The cadets are then ranked by order of merit and sorted according to their majors (technical, foreign language, nursing, and non-STEM). The number of technical majors accepted is based on the needs of both the rated and nonrated communities (plus an attrition factor); likewise, the number of foreign language majors accepted is based on current needs (plus an attrition factor).[3] All qualified nurses who face the board are accepted because the demand for nurses is high. AFROTC's steady-state production target is 2,000 officers, but 2,410 cadets were selected for the POC in FY 2013 to account for attrition. Once chosen for the POC, selectees must satisfactorily complete field training that occurs the summer after selection and sign a contract.

One factor that needs to be accounted for is the number of cadets selected for rated AFSCs. AFROTC allows all interested cadets the opportunity to compete for rated career fields. Approximately 250 AFROTC cadets in technical degree programs get classified into a rated AFSC each year.[4] Thus, the commissioning source must account for the nonrated technical accession requirements, the percentage of cadets with technical degrees who get classified into a rated AFSC, and attrition in the technical field of study when determining scholarship offers and forecasting commissioning production. This is important because the Holm Center (and AFROTC in particular) is relied on to produce enough cadets with technical degrees to fill the majority of nonrated technical-degreed career field requirements.

Historical AFROTC Scholarship Production Against Current Education Requirements

The current AFROTC scholarship process does not address the relationship between requirements and scholarships except for the critical technical degrees (meteorology, computer engineering, electrical engineering, nuclear engineering, and nuclear physics) and does not address how the numbers of technical and foreign language scholarships for HSSP and ICSP are determined. Our understanding is that the current AFROTC scholarship process emphasizes

---

[3] The number of technical majors accepted accounts for the number of cadets earning technical degrees who volunteered for rated duty in recent years plus the current needs of nonrated technical degrees.

[4] Statistic provided by Col (ret) Frederick Guendel, former deputy registrar of AFROTC/RR, 2010.

degrees perceived to have top priority or to have, anecdotally, been difficult to produce. As a result, critical technical degrees,[5] technical degrees, foreign language degrees, and nursing degrees have overall priority. As we stated earlier, there is no direct link between degrees and AFSCs (for the nonmandatory education requirements), making specific degree requirements hard to determine. Thus, it is difficult to assess the number and type of degrees AFROTC should be producing. We recommend an exploration of how scholarship offers can be derived from requirements. A simple schema for establishing the relationship is to determine, for example, how many total new engineers of a particular type are needed each year and then estimate how many will be produced by USAFA and OTS, how many will be produced by AFROTC without the incentive of a scholarship, and how many engineers will be diverted to rated career fields. Any predicted shortages may need to be made up by offering scholarships. Ideally, this analysis should be done at the shred (that is, assigning officers to specific engineering disciplines within the larger career) level of disaggregation rather than at the career field level.[6]

AFROTC Scholarship Analysis

AFROTC has been executing its scholarship program with little direction from AF/A1 on the types of degrees needed to satisfy accession sustainment requirements and without guidance on the analysis required to evaluate how the program has been performing. Therefore, we were asked to evaluate the effectiveness of the AFROTC scholarship policy toward meeting Air Force nonrated line officer accession education requirements and to provide a methodology for calculating how many cadets AFROTC should aim to graduate with various degrees to better meet accession education requirements.

We asked for a wide range of data that would show every cadet's involvement with the AFROTC scholarship program, starting from receiving an AFROTC scholarship offer (whether accepted or declined) to commissioning into the Air Force.[7] We received less data than desired, and the data we did receive were inconsistent or incomplete, which limited the scope of the analysis we were able to conduct. Had we received all the data we requested, we could have analyzed a wide range of policy issues, including ROI and potentially to optimize how to allocate scholarship funds to get the largest ROI while still meeting accession education requirements. This leads to one of our first recommendations: For AFROTC to analyze and evaluate its scholarship policy and future ROI, it ought to be maintaining the kinds of data we requested in a central or single repository, likely at HQ AFROTC. When we originally requested these data, we

---

[5] AFROTC has a list of critical technical degrees (meteorology, computer engineering, electrical engineering, nuclear engineering, and nuclear physics), but how these degrees were deemed critical is not clear.

[6] In these computations, AFROTC production equates to commissioning, while USAFA and OTS production equates to both commissioning and accessing (they occur simultaneously).

[7] Appendix B provides detailed information on the data requested; data received; and if received, the usable data.

were informed that not all are located or managed at HQ AFROTC. Some of the data are kept at the detachment level, thereby providing further evidence that the data are not kept with an eye to scholarship production analysis. The data had also not previously been brought together for this kind of analysis. To our knowledge, the data set we sought to assemble is novel and is the first attempt to analyze the degree to which AFROTC historical scholarship production meets the education needs of the Air Force.

We could not conduct the full range of analysis we had hoped for, so we narrowed our scope to determining whether AFROTC scholarship production was sufficient to meet AFSC education requirements by using the sustainment and dynamic requirements contained in the sustainment PGL from AF/A1PF, given OTS and USAFA production. Such an analysis will likely need to be conducted annually as career fields define their accession education requirements or, more specifically, change their AFOCD accession education requirements.[8]

The data we did receive from AFROTC included whether the cadet dropped, disenrolled, or was commissioned, as well as various scholarship information, such as tuition, major, whether the scholarship contract was terminated or completed, and length and type of scholarship. We then merged this AFROTC data set with officer master personnel files from AFPC. Given the data limitations discussed earlier, we narrowed the merged data set to include a record for every cadet or trainee who had been commissioned from AFROTC, OTS, and USAFA from 2005 to 2013 and the SOC, the undergraduate degree earned, the commission year, and the initially assigned AFSC (assigned through the classification process). Even with the narrowed data set, we had to address a number of issues to produce a coherent set of data for commissioned cadets from 2005–2013.[9]

The comprehensive data set contained 30,401 cadets who had been commissioned from AFROTC, OTS, and USAFA from FYs 2005 through 2013 and that had an entry for SOC, commission year, undergraduate degree, and initially assigned AFSC. Figure 7.1 shows the

---

[8] During the writing of this document, an AF/A1 tasking was issued to each career field to justify (and in justifying, validate or refine) its education requirements in terms of undergraduate academic degrees.

[9] The issues with the data were as follows:

- SOC and commission year were missing for some AFROTC cadets. Either this information was simply missing or the cadet had not yet made it into the officer master personnel files, but the data were present in the AFROTC data set. This was mostly an issue for cadets who commissioned in 2012 through 2014.
- Undergraduate academic degree information was missing for some cadets from all SOCs, mostly for medical and rated personnel. This information was missing from the master personnel files but was sometimes present in the AFROTC data set when the cadet had a scholarship. Thus, we were able to backfill many AFROTC cadets' missing degrees. OTS commissionees had significantly more missing academic degrees, likely highlighting a data collection issue and/or gap in the process.
- The initially assigned AFSC was missing for some cadets. This information was missing from the initial AFSC variable, but we were able to fill in the variable from another variable in the data set that provided a primary AFSC. This was mostly an issue for nonline AFSCs.

Figure 7.1. Air Force Commission Production, FYs 2005–2013

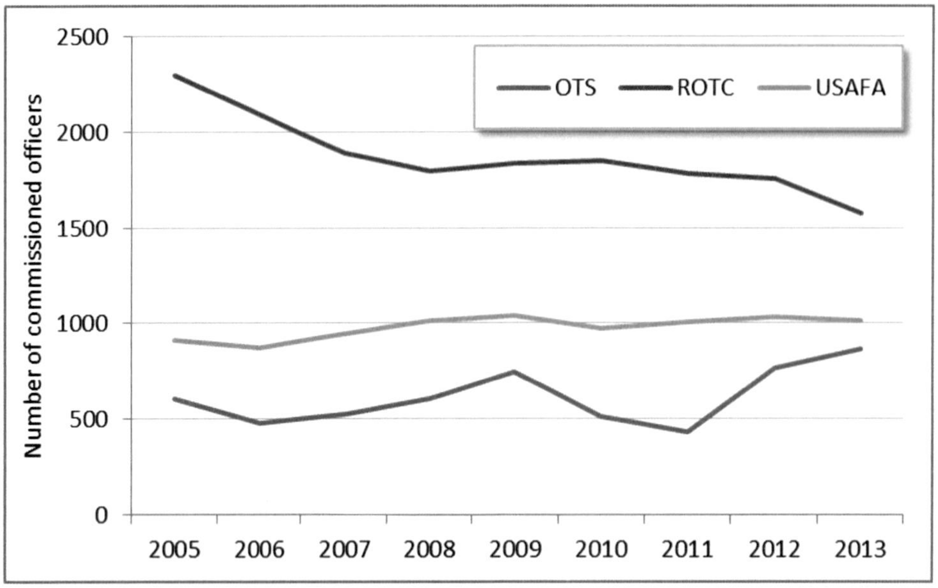

commission production from 2005–2013 for the three main commissioning sources. We used this comprehensive data set to calculate annual historical production for OTS and USAFA, as well as annual historical scholarship and nonscholarship AFROTC production.

To be able to compare historical production against sustainment requirements, we asked AF/A1PF for what we refer to as the sustainment PGL for FYs 2005–2013. The sustainment PGL contains the accession requirements by three-digit AFSC, which includes line (rated and nonrated) and nonline sustainment accession requirement. We were looking for two kinds of data in the sustainment PGL: the sustainment requirement (steady-state accession requirement over time required to maintain the health of the career field) and the dynamic requirement (a beginning-of-execution-year target that incorporates end strength, previous year's accessions, and an acceptable level of risk toward future career field health). A dynamic requirement typically differs from the sustainment requirement and is usually lower, unless the AFSC is considered critical (and is therefore shielded from reductions). Although we had asked for FY 2005–2013 sustainment data, creating a complete set of data took additional work and assumptions and merging several data sources. Thus, the sustainment and dynamic requirement data set for FYs 2005–2014 is likely a novel data set.

Methodology for Calculating AFROTC Scholarship Production

Ideally, aggregate commission production should be such that aggregate sustainment requirements are met with potentially a small overage to account for attrition between commissioning and the completion of initial skills training.[10] Attrition most often occurs when cadets have been classified into a rated AFSC; for example, an officer being classified into the pilot career field but then being disqualified because he or she loses consciousness during certain aircraft maneuvers. For clarification, when we say *production* we mean *commissioning production*. Therefore, we have the following relationship:

$$\textit{Sustainment Requirement} \leq \textit{AFROTC production} + \textit{OTS production} + \textit{USAFA production}.$$

Also, our sponsors are concerned about AFROTC scholarship production, so we disaggregated the AFROTC data into scholarship and nonscholarship production. Using the following relationship can determine whether AFROTC scholarship production is sufficient, given OTS and USAFA production, to meet aggregate sustainment requirements:

$$\textit{AFROTC production} = \textit{AFROTC scholarship production} + \textit{AFROTC nonscholarship production}.$$

Plugging the AFROTC production equation into our overall equation and solving for AFROTC scholarship production gives the following:≥

$$\textit{AFROTC scholarship production} \geq \max\,\{\textit{Sustainment Requirement} - \textit{AFROTC nonscholarship production} - \textit{OTS production} - \textit{USAFA production}, 0\}$$

Results

We present the results using two data sets: aggregate requirements and line requirements.[11] The aggregate set includes both line (rated and nonrated) and nonline officer production (officers classified into the medical, dental, nursing, chaplain, or legal career fields). The delta referred to in Figure 7.2 (also shown in Figures 7.3–7.11 for particular academic disciplines) is actual AFROTC scholarship production in a given FY minus projected AFROTC scholarship production (as explained in the equation above) that would have been required to meet sustainment or dynamic requirements. The projected AFROTC scholarship production uses two different averaging schemes in which the historical commissioning production is averaged to provide two different projections of FY 2014 AFROTC scholarship commissioning production. Thus, if the delta is negative, AFROTC scholarship (commissioning) production was not sufficient to meet requirements; if the delta is positive, AFROTC scholarship (commissioning) production was sufficient to meet requirements. Using the equations above and historical data, we calculated that AFROTC scholarship production levels have not been sufficient to meet

[10] In this context, *attrition* refers to officers who wash out of training for various reasons but are likely to remain in the military and be reclassified into a different career field via a process separate from the initial classification discussed in this document. During force-shaping years, it is not a given that an officer who washes out of training will remain in the force.

[11] We are missing the nonline dynamic requirements for FY 2005–2007, so this discussion starts with the aggregate dynamic requirements and assumes that the FY 2005–2007 nonline dynamic requirements are equal to those for FY 2008. Then we remove all the nonline data and present only the AFROTC line scholarship production needed to meet the line officer dynamic requirements.

sustainment or dynamic requirements in the aggregate (including line and nonline officer production, rated and nonrated production, and across all career fields and academic degrees), as shown in Figure 7.2. Focusing only on line sustainment and dynamic requirements, Figure 7.3 shows that historical AFROTC scholarship production has been insufficient but that production was on track to meet the FY 2014 line sustainment and dynamic requirements. It is not surprising that AFROTC scholarship production is less than sustainment requirements because dynamic requirements are given as the execution-year target.

The FY 2014 calculations provide two methods for forecasting how well the projected AFROTC scholarship production would have met meet the 2014 line sustainment and dynamic requirements either in aggregate across all career fields or academic degrees that align to one career field. The two methods provide two means of determining whether projected scholarship production will be under or over at the beginning of the execution year, thereby potentially discovering any academic degree shortages that will need to be remedied in the execution year. The first method uses a weighted average of FYs 2005–2013 historical commissioning production and user-driven weights, and the second method uses the typical historical average of FY 2005–2013 commissioning production; both methods allow this comparison in whichever category is being considered (aggregate across all career fields or academic degrees that align to one career field). The weighted average calculation weights recent years more heavily than earlier years because the current state has been greatly influenced by recent events. Table 7.3 gives the weights assigned to the years in the data range.

Figures 7.2 through 7.11 show the results of scholarship production with respect to production requirements, displaying the difference between what was desired and what was achieved. The values are negative when the production requirement was not met and are positive when it was exceeded. The lack of a bar indicates that production exactly met the requirement.

Table 7.3. Weights Used in Calculating Weighted Average

FY	Weight
2005	0.50
2006	0.50
2007	0.50
2008	0.50
2009	0.75
2010	1.00
2011	1.00
2012	1.25
2013	1.50

Figure 7.2. Success of AFROTC Historical Scholarship Production in Meeting Aggregate and Dynamic Sustainment Requirements

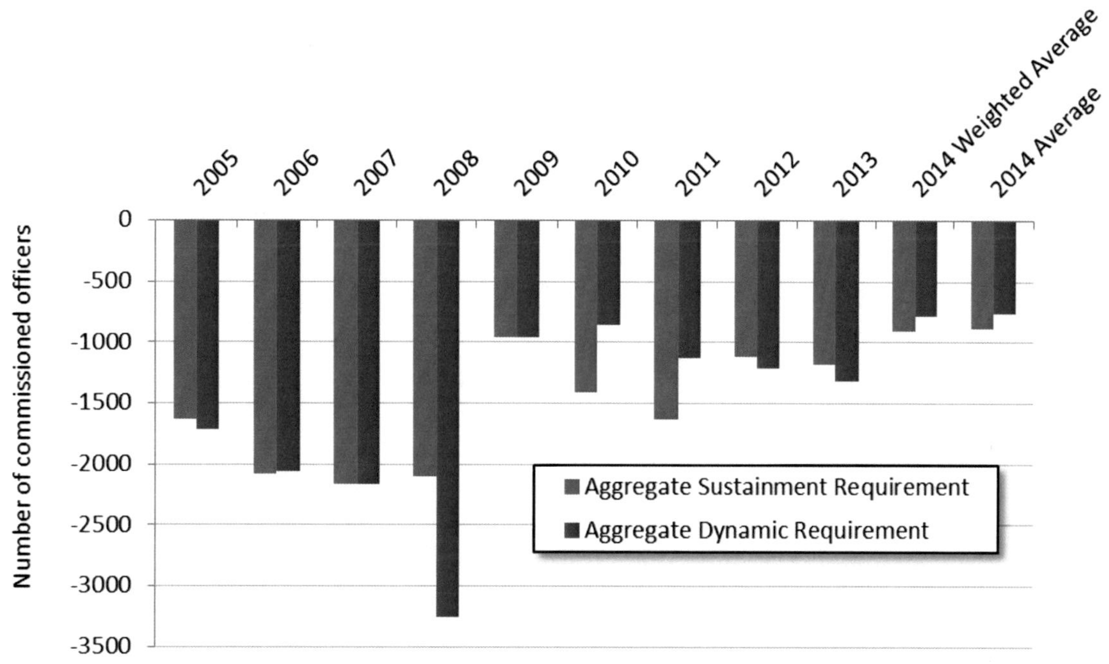

Figure 7.3. Success of AFROTC Historical Scholarship Production Line Sustainment and Dynamic Requirements for Line Officers

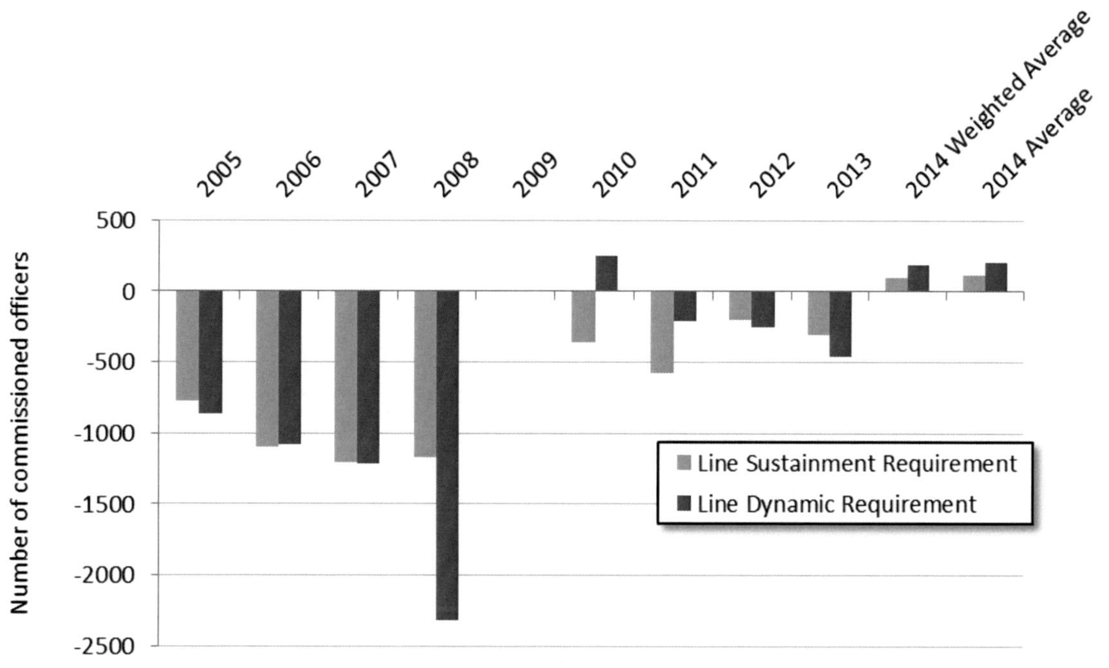

Production requirements refers to the number of officers who were supposed to commission in a given FY; therefore, a negative delta means a shortage of commissioned officers, and a positive delta means a surplus. During the writing of this document, actual FY 2014 scholarship production was unknown, so we provided a method for forecasting AFROTC's ability to meet commissioning requirements through its scholarship program.

Because our sponsors are most concerned about meeting nonrated line officer sustainment requirements, we further disaggregated the data to address these requirements. An additional area of concern is meeting the engineering requirement and newly emerging STEM requirements (such as recently changed academic requirements for Cyberspace Operations [17D] and an OR requirement within Personnel [38P]); thus, we further disaggregate the data to investigate these engineering and STEM requirements. Last, we analyzed meteorology requirements because this is one of AFROTC's critical technical degrees and because, as we were writing this document, USAFA had proposed closing down its meteorology department. Subsequent figures present the results for engineering, computer science, meteorology, and OR degree production, as well as overproduction of other degrees, based on the classification analysis discussed in Section 4 and using the same methodology that produced Figures 7.2 and 7.3.

However, the issue is more complex because the sustainment PGL is created by determining requirements for each career field, while our analysis considers degree production. Not all degrees align with specific career fields, making it harder to determine whether degree production satisfactorily meets the requirements when considering degree production by number and kind. We can accurately discuss engineering and meteorology because these types of degrees specifically align with the engineering and meteorology career fields, respectively. However, that is not the case for computer science and OR; while these degrees are appropriate for Cyberspace (17D) and Operations Research Analyst (61A), respectively, these career fields also seek officers with other degrees. Also, as stated earlier, given the way education requirements are expressed in the AFOCD, it is much harder to determine degree production requirements because the education requirements do not provide a priority; percentage needed; and whether the degrees are mandatory, desired, or permitted.

Before showing the results, we will provide the methodology once more, given that the focus is now on nonrated line production, which includes cadets who received AFROTC scholarships but were assigned to rated career fields. The following equation shows how we calculated a lower bound on AFROTC engineering scholarship production:

$$\begin{gathered}\textit{AFROTC eng scholarship production} \geq \max\ \{\textit{NRL eng Sustainment Requirement} \\ -\ \textit{AFROTC NRL eng nonscholarship production} - \textit{OTS NRL eng production} \\ -\ \textit{USAFA NRL eng production} + \textit{AFROTC rated eng scholarship production},\ 0\}\end{gathered}$$

where *eng* is engineering with and *NRL is* nonrated line with *NRL*. We calculated other academic fields and degrees and linked career fields using the same methodology. We calculated historical deltas for the engineering career fields (civil engineering and developmental engineers) as actual AFROTC engineering scholarship production minus AFROTC engineering scholarship production, as specified in the equation, and made one calculation for sustainment requirements and another for dynamic requirements. The equation considers all officers who commissioned between FYs 2005 and 2013 and earned an engineering degree, as defined by the academic specialty code attached to the degree. As an example, USAFA nonrated line engineering production is the historic average of USAFA cadets to have commissioned from FYs 2005–2013, earned an engineering degree as specified by academic specialty code, and were assigned to a nonrated line career field. Likewise, the equation also calculates historical averages for all other production variables. The nonrated line engineer sustainment requirement is the sum of the civil engineering and developmental engineer sustainment requirements in a given FY.

Figure 7.4 shows that, historically, AFROTC scholarship production fell short (as indicated by a negative delta) of sustainment and dynamic requirements until FY 2009. It might seem that there is excess engineering production in more recent years, but the engineering requirement captured is only for civil and developmental engineers (the mandatory engineering career fields). The excess-to-requirements engineering production allows engineers to be classified into other career fields that desire officers with engineering degrees. With the AFOCD education entry requirements as currently expressed, it is hard to identify a total numerical engineering

Figure 7.4. Success of AFROTC Scholarship Production in Meeting Requirements for Engineering Officers

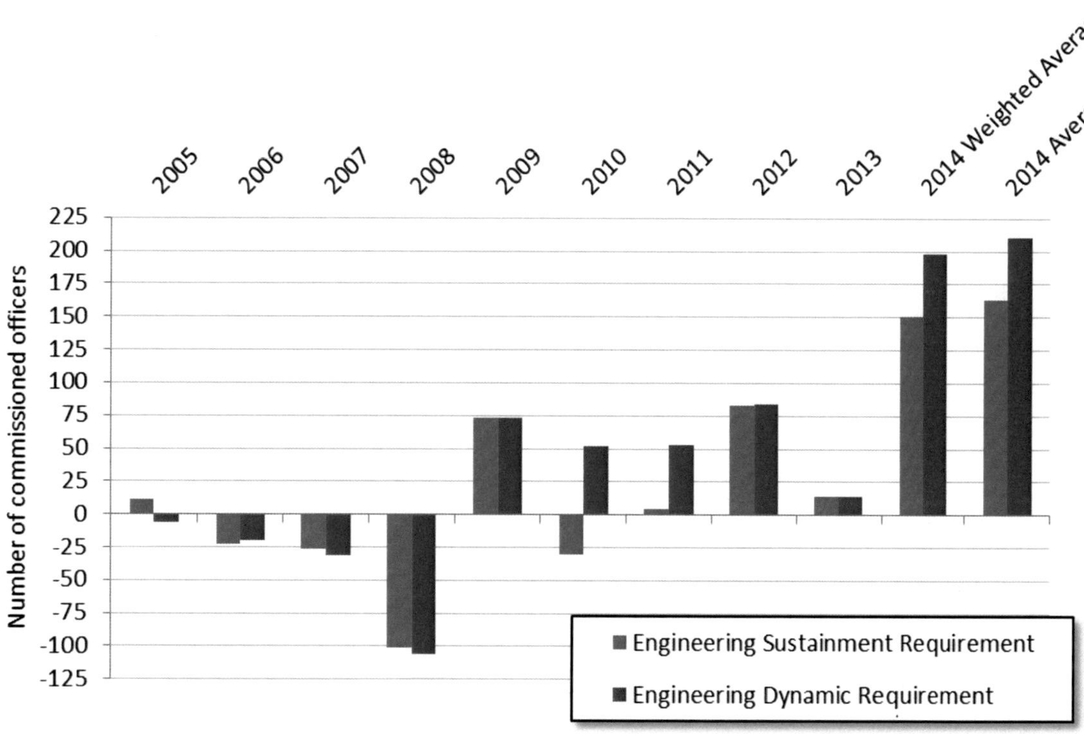

requirement and to know whether the AFROTC engineering production is meeting both the mandatory and desired degree requirements. Once the AFOCD education requirement paragraphs are exchanged for the education matrices, a total numerical requirement could be determined, and an assessment could be made of whether the engineering degree production is sufficient to meet both mandatory and desired degree requirements. Given historical scholarship production, the projected FY 2014 AFROTC engineering scholarship production was going to exceed sustainment and dynamic requirements (as indicated by the large positive delta). Barring recent AFROTC scholarship processes making any significant departure from historical trends, FY 2014 commissionees should have allowed the classification model to better meet desired engineering degree requirements in other nonengineering career fields.

Figure 7.5 also shows that AFROTC meteorology scholarship production was insufficient to meet the requirements for the Weather (15W) career field from FYs 2005–2013 but is projected to meet the FY 2014 dynamic requirement by a couple of officers. These calculations show that the Air Force has not been meeting the meteorology accession requirement for many years, and this problem would be exacerbated if USAFA closed its meteorology department (see Figure 7.6). Although USAFA has produced only a handful of cadets with meteorology degrees for the last several years, USAFA meteorology production still helped mitigate the shortfall of

Figure 7.5. Success of AFROTC Scholarship Production in Meeting Requirements for Meteorology Officers

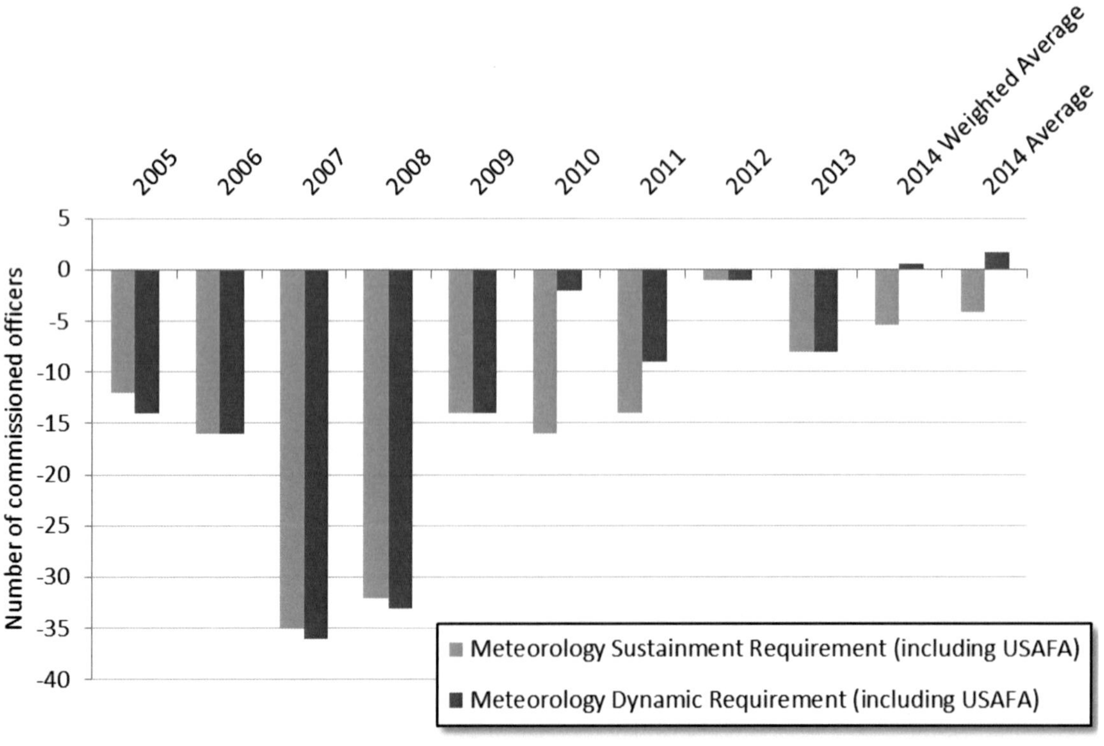

Figure 7.6. Success in Meeting Requirement for Meteorology Graduates With and Without USAFA Contribution

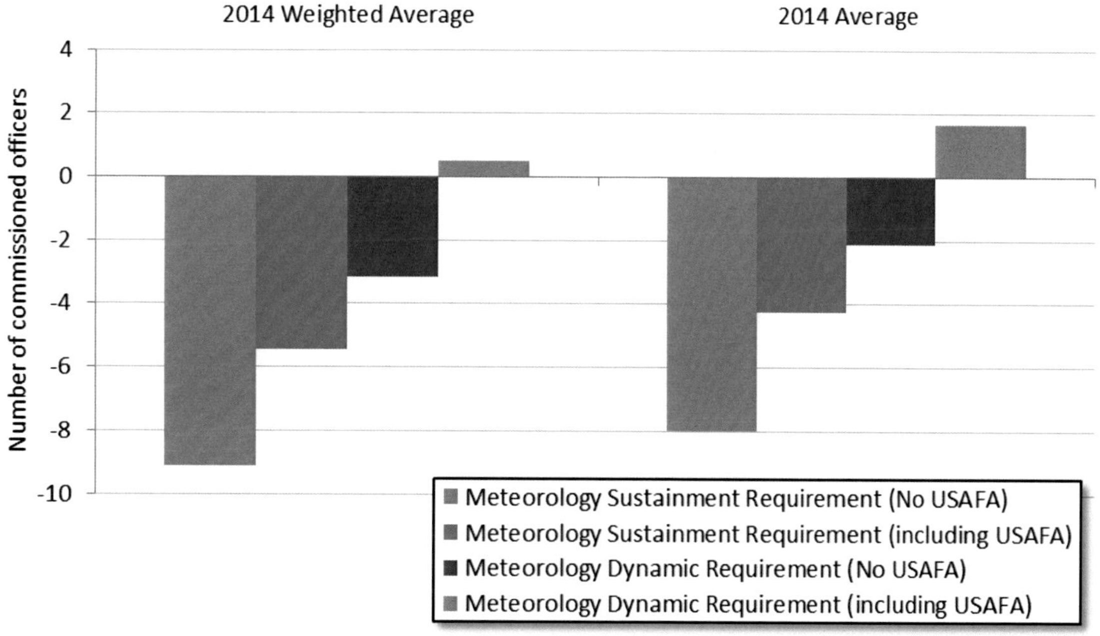

meteorology degreed officers for the weather career field, as shown by the teal and orange bars (when compared to the green and purple bars, respectively). If USAFA does close its meteorology department, AFROTC will have to intensify and likely modify its recruiting efforts to attract and retain more cadets who wish to enter into the weather career field.

The Cyberspace Operations (17D) CFM recently changed the field's education entry requirements to strengthen the language to try to obtain officers who have degrees more in line with its mission, such as computer science or information assurance. In this vein, our analysis looked at whether AFROTC computer science or information assurance scholarship production has been sufficient since FY 2012 (the first usage of the combined classification model) to meet 40 percent of the total 17D accession requirement. The 40 percent is not a requirement in the classification model but, rather, is the actual percentage of cadets with computer science or information assurance degrees assigned to the cyberspace career field out of its total target in the last two years. Because this is an actual result of the classification model and because the model has not changed significantly from FYs 2012 to 2014, it seems appropriate to use 40 percent as the computer science or information assurance benchmark. Figure 7.7 shows that, in FYs 2012 and 2013, AFROTC computer science or information assurance scholarship production was insufficient (as indicated by the negative delta) to meet 40 percent of the 17D requirement. AFROTC is projected to fall short of the FY 2014 requirement as well. Because the Air Force has not been commissioning enough computer scientists to meet 40 percent of the 17D requirement, other career fields are unlikely to receive officers with computer science degrees.

Figure 7.7. Success of AFROTC Computer Science or Information Assurance Scholarship Production in Meeting 17D Requirement

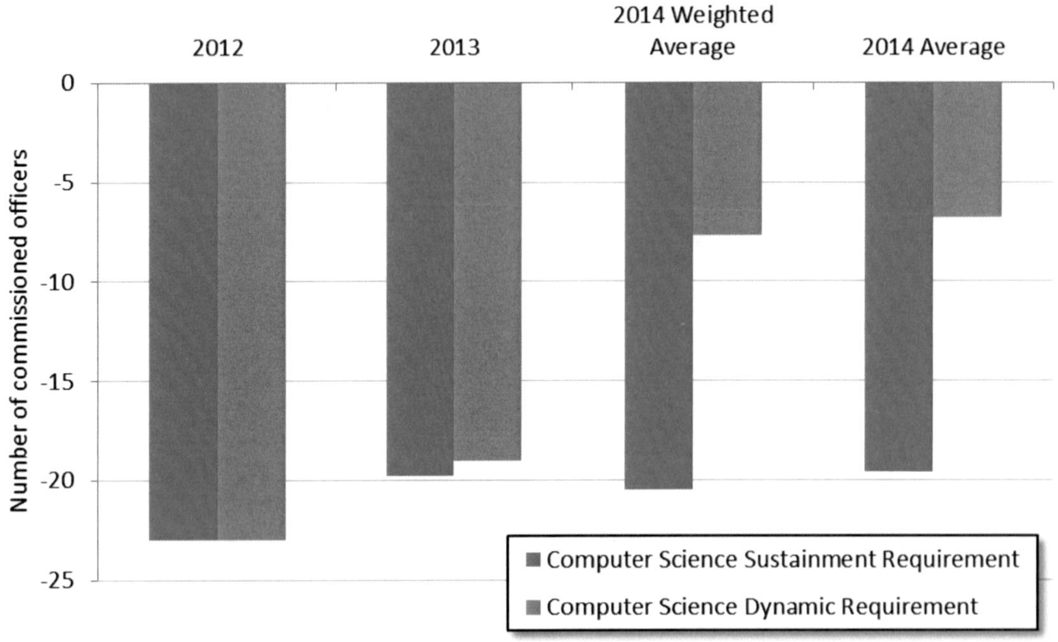

Both the Operations Analyst (61A) and Personnel (38P) CFMs have recently changed the AFOCD education entry requirements, which will result in more operations researchers and operations analysts being classified into 61A and 38P to meet requirements. Managers of 38P have stated that 25 percent of their accession requirement is to be filled with cadets having earned OR, IE, or mathematics degrees. The 61A CFM recently tightened the 61A education entry requirement; as a result, most economics degrees no longer qualify to fill the OR requirement. As these changes come into effect for the FY 2015 classification, AFROTC should make OR degrees a high recruiting priority. Figure 7.8 shows that AFROTC OR scholarship production was insufficient in FY 2012 but exceeded requirements in FY 2013 (when the higher OR requirement was not in place). To calculate the future OR requirement for FY 2014, we assumed that cadets with OR degrees would satisfy 25 percent of the 38P OR, IE, and mathematics requirement and 25 percent of the 61A OR, IE, and mathematics requirement. We made this assumption because, of the total supply of cadets with degrees satisfying both the 38P and 61A OR, IE, and mathematics requirements, 25 percent had OR degrees; 56 percent had mathematics degrees; and 19 percent had IE degrees. Because the supply of cadets is not likely to change drastically from one year to the next, we assumed production percentages would be similar. Given this assumption, AFROTC OR scholarship production is projected to be short (as indicated by the negative delta) in FY 2014 from sustainment and dynamic requirements when considering the new 25 percent OR requirement in 38P Personnel. However, Figure 7.8 obscures the fact that USAFA has essentially been the main producer of OR degrees for the Air Force, as

Figure 7.8. Success of AFROTC Operations Research Scholarship Production in Meeting Operations Research Requirements

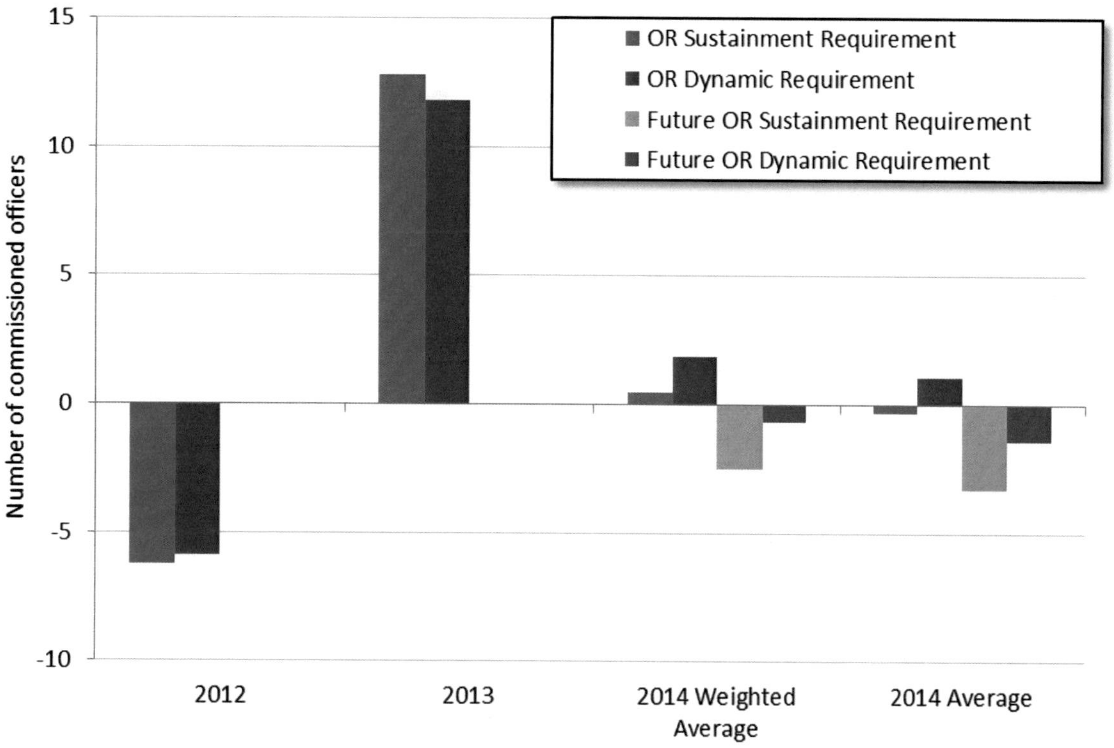

shown in Figure 7.9. If USAFA did not produce enough, the Air Force fell short of the requirement. But the true demand for OR degrees is opaque. Technically, all requirements would be met if the Air Force commissioned enough cadets who had earned either IE or mathematics degrees to satisfy both 38P and 61A. It is therefore possible to argue that zero OR production does not mean that there is or has been a shortage of OR degrees. While the new education matrices will give a more clear demand signal, it still will not provide a hard target for OR degrees because, rom the CFMs perspective, IE and mathematics degrees are equivalent.

Finally, AFROTC produces several degrees in excess (as indicated by the positive delta): History, foreign language, political science, and criminal justice or criminology degrees are desired by only one career field each and that at less than 100 percent. According to the FY 2014 classification data,

- Cadets with history degrees cadets comprised 10 percent of Intelligence (14N) classification.
- Foreign language cadets comprised 8 percent of Intelligence (14N) classification.
- Political science cadets comprised 29 percent of Intelligence (14N) classification.
- Criminal justice or criminology cadets comprised 35 percent of Security Forces (31P) requirement.

Figure 7.9. USAFA Nonrated Line OR Production

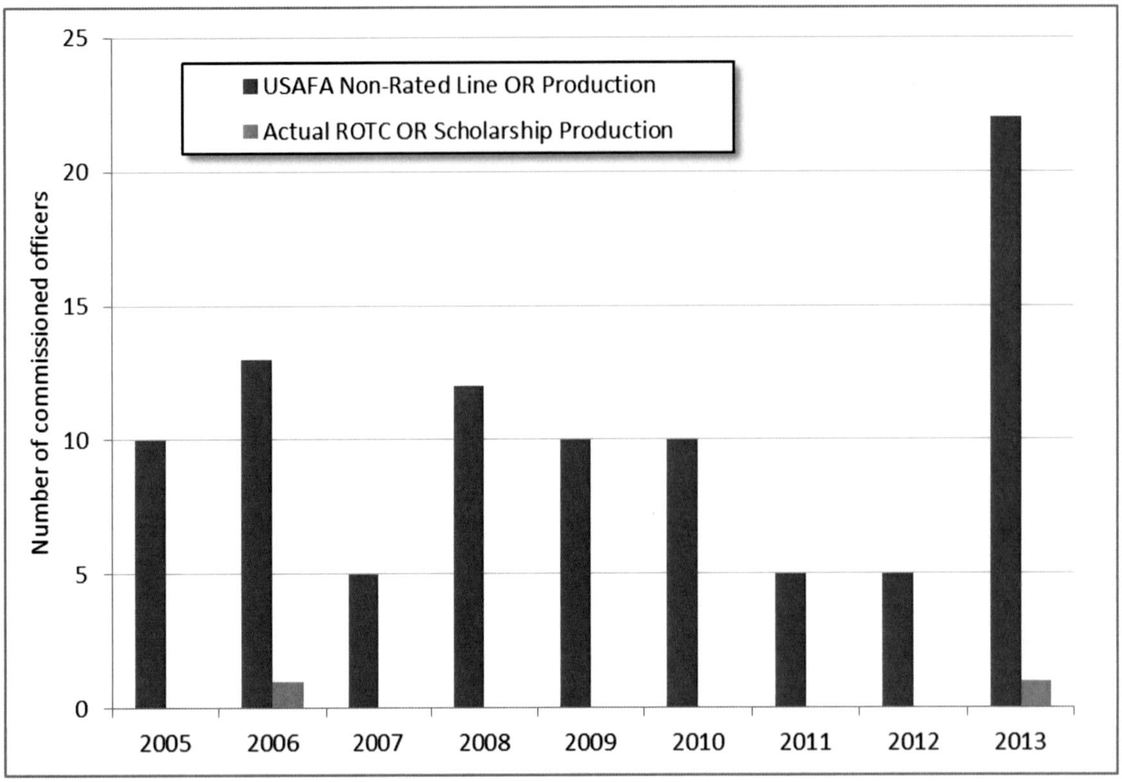

NOTE: The Nonrated Line OR Production was almost exclusively from USAFA. For the period presented, OTS and AFROTC produced only three OR accessions over the nine years.

As Figure 7.10 shows, given these assumptions for the four degrees and two career fields, AFROTC scholarship production is in excess of the requirements for these fields. In FYs 2012 and 2013, actual production of scholarships in history, foreign language, political science, and criminal justice exceeded 10 percent of the 14N sustainment and dynamic requirement (for history, foreign language, and political science) and exceeded 35 percent of the 31P sustainment and dynamic requirement (hence the positive delta). Using the historical production in each of these academic disciplines and accounting for 10 or 35 percent (as appropriate) of the sustainment and dynamic requirements in FY 2014 for 14N and 31P, respectively, projected AFROTC scholarship production in these four academic disciplines is going to exceed the requirement.

Figure 7.10. History, Foreign Language, Political Science, and Criminal Justice Degrees Produced in Excess of 31P and 14N Desired Degree Requirements

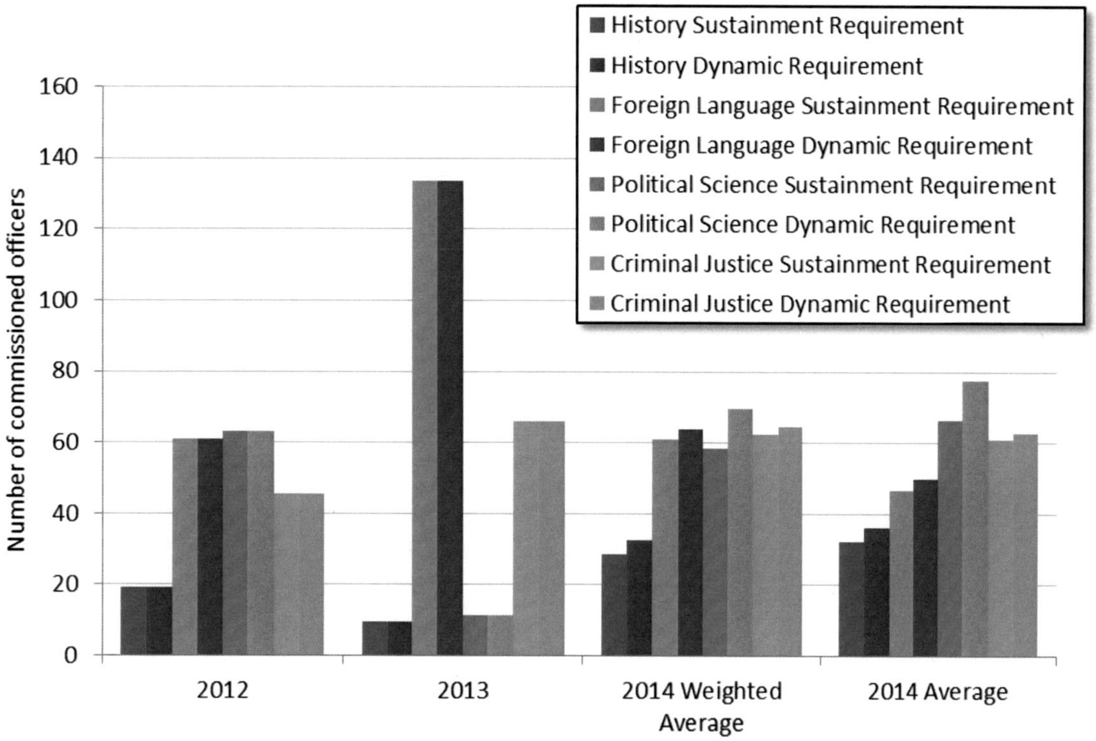

NOTE: The chart displays the difference between the requirement and the production for the disciplines listed. Were the production to fall short, the bar would be negative.

Figure 7.11 shows that, for history, foreign language, political science, and criminal justice or criminology degrees, the magnitude of AFROTC scholarship production has directly contributed to the excess production. For history, political science, and criminal justice or criminology, we propose curtailing the excessive scholarship production and instead giving the scholarships to competitive individuals seeking to earn degrees in more-technical fields, such as computer science and OR, or other kinds of degrees desirable to one, or preferably more, career. With respect to the foreign language degrees, the results are misleading because there are undocumented AF/A1D foreign language requirements that are crosscutting and not linked to any particular career field. Thus, there is a need for foreign language degrees, but the system does not know the magnitude of the requirement and therefore cannot determine if it is being met.

Figure 7.11. AFROTC FY 2014 Projected Scholarship Production Compared to Dynamic Requirements

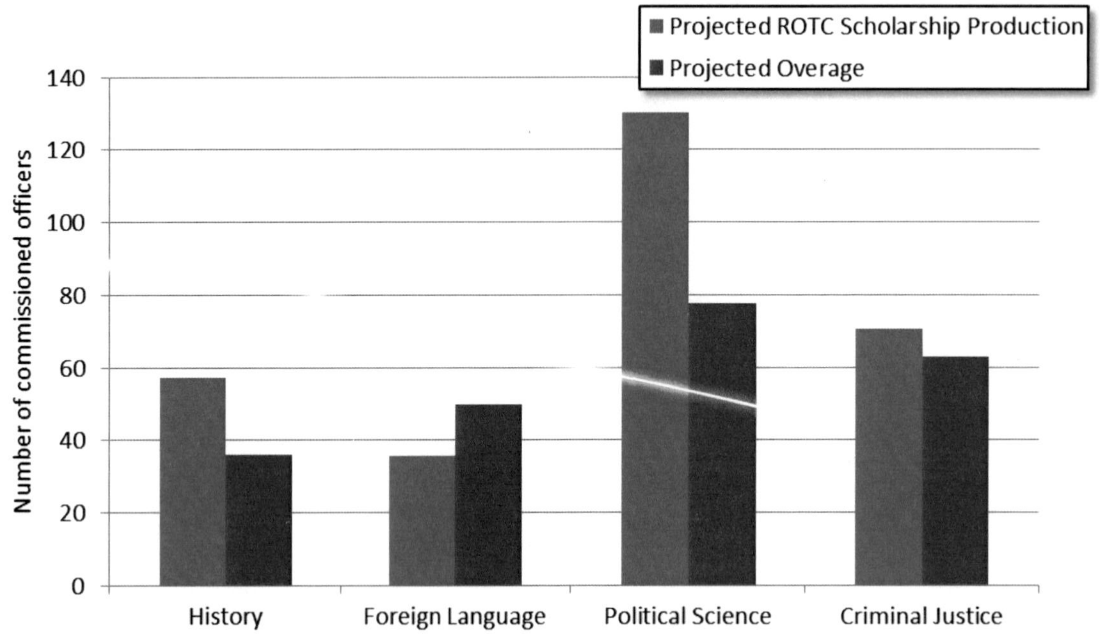

NOTE: the FY 2014 average dynamic requirement is based on 10 percent of the 14N FY 2014 dynamic requirement (for history, foreign language, and political science) and 35 percent of the 31P FY 2014 dynamic requirement (for criminal justice).

Recommendations

In summary, we recommend the following:

- AFROTC engineering scholarship production is healthy, and the policies and practices enabling this level of production should continue because the current apparent excess is actually fulfilling undocumented desirable engineering requirements.
- To ensure meeting the meteorology requirement, AFROTC meteorology scholarship production will need to increase to offset the decrease in USAFA production (should USAFA close its meteorology program), thereby increasing the importance of meteorology as a critical technical degree.
- AFROTC computer science or information assurance scholarship production will need to increase to meet the needs of the 17D career field and to meet emerging computer science requirements in other career fields.
- AFROTC OR production will need to increase to meet the new OR demands in the 61A and 38P career fields. Because AFROTC production has essentially been zero, this recommendation effectively means adding OR degrees to the critical technical degree recruiting list and ensuring that the Air Force has detachments at or cross-town relationships with universities and colleges that offer an OR degree.

- AFROTC should offer fewer scholarships to cadets seeking to earn degrees in history, political science, and criminal justice or criminology and redirect these scholarship funds to cadets seeking more-technical or STEM degrees to help meet education entry requirements (both mandatory and desired).
- AFROTC should continue to offer scholarships to cadets earning degrees in foreign languages to help meet the cross-functional requirements documented by AF/A1D.
- AF/A1D should document the foreign language requirements in the sustainment PGL, and the Air Force should think through linking foreign language degree production to meet cross-functional requirements, as well as meeting foreign language requirements in the 14N career field.

Appendix A. Model Formulation—Determining Aggregate Education Requirements by Academic Degree Type

This appendix provides the details of the optimization model described in Section 6 to evaluate whether an accession cohort meets career field requirements and for developing aggregate academic degree targets. The model minimizes the difference between the academic degrees the Air Force accesses on average and the degrees in the solution while, at the same time, satisfying the requirements that the CFMs have expressed in the education requirement matrices. One way to arrive at such a solution is to solve for $x_{i,j,k}$, given the constraints for the number of accessions in each AFSC and tier and, at the same, time minimizing the difference between the solution and what the Air Force is currently accessing.

Looking at the education matrix for each AFSC with its prioritized tiers and specific degree types, let $x_{i,j,k}$ be the number of officer accessions for degree i in AFSC j and requirement tier k ($i = 1, \dots n$ degree types; $j = 1, \dots m$ NRL AFSCs; $k = 1, \dots p$ possible tiers). Given information about the total number of accessions in each AFSC, we can set aj, k as the required number of accessions in AFSC j, tier k based on the percentages in each tier for each AFSC's education matrix. Then, define $b_{i,j,k}$ as a binary variable that is "1" when degree i is acceptable for AFSC j, tier k and "0" otherwise.

With these variables and constraints, it may be tempting to solve for $x_{i,j,k}$ to determine exactly how many officers should be accessed in each degree type. However, because so many possible degree types can satisfy each AFSC and tier, the overall system of constraints is not sufficient to determine the best among the many possible values of the variable $x_{i,j,k}$. These constraints could be used to test an accession scheme to see whether it satisfies the degree requirements for each AFSC or whether changes to the types of degrees accessed will meet requirements.

The Air Force has been and is currently able to access officers in certain degree types, and these accession degrees satisfy many if not all of the education requirements the CFMs have defined. It may not be necessary to radically change the types of degrees accessed. It might not be necessary to expend resources to recruit and access radically different degree types. Therefore, we seek a solution that differs as little as possible from current accession degrees types but still satisfies the requirements the CFMs have expressed in their education requirement matrices. One way to arrive at such a solution is to minimize how much the required number of accessions in each degree type differs from what is currently being accessed:

$$min \sum_{i=1}^{n} \left| \sum_{j=1}^{m} \sum_{k=1}^{p} x_{i,j,k} - c_i \right|,$$

where c_i is the current number of accessions for degree type i. For satisfying the degree requirements for each tier in each AFSC, the constraint is

$$\sum_{i=1}^{n} b_{i,j,k} x_{i,j,k} \geq a_{j,k} \ \forall j,k.$$

And since not every education matrix completely defines the numbers in each AFSC, an additional constraint is required to ensure the solution provides enough accessions for each AFSC:

$$\sum_{k=1}^{p} \sum_{i=1}^{n} b_{i,j,k} x_{i,j,k} = \sum_{k=1}^{p} a_{j,k} \ \forall j.$$

The number of accessions in each degree, AFSC, and tier cannot be negative:

$$x_{i,j,k} \geq 0 \ \forall i,j,k.$$

The presence of the absolute value in the objective function means it is not possible to directly apply linear programming. However, observing that min|x| is equivalent to

$$\min t$$

$$t \geq x$$

$$t \geq -x.$$

We can introduce n variables, t_i to transform the problem to a linear program. The complete objective function is now

$$\min \sum_{i=1}^{n} t_i,$$

subject to

$$\left|\sum_{j=1}^{m} \sum_{k=1}^{p} x_{i,j,k} - c_i\right| \leq t_i \qquad \forall i = 1, \ldots p,$$

which is equivalent to the two constraints:

$$\sum_{j=1}^{m} \sum_{k=1}^{p} x_{i,j,k} - c_i \leq t_i \qquad \forall i = 1, \ldots p$$

$$-\sum_{j=1}^{m} \sum_{k=1}^{p} x_{i,j,k} + c_i \leq t_i \qquad \forall i = 1, \ldots p.$$

Therefore, the entire problem formulation is

$$\min \sum_{i=1}^{n} t_i,$$

subject to

$$\sum_{j=1}^{m} \sum_{k=1}^{p} x_{i,j,k} - c_i \leq t_i \qquad \forall i$$

$$-\sum_{j=1}^{m} \sum_{k=1}^{p} x_{i,j,k} + c_i \leq t_i \qquad \forall i$$

$$\sum_{i=1}^{n} b_{i,j,k} x_{i,j,k} \geq a_{j,k} \qquad \forall j,k$$

$$\sum_{k=1}^{p} \sum_{i=1}^{n} x_{i,j,k} = \sum_{k=1}^{p} a_{j,k} \qquad \forall j$$

$$x_{i,j,k} \geq 0 \qquad \forall i,j,k.$$

Appendix B. AFROTC Scholarship Data Requested and Received

Table B.1 shows the data we initially asked for from AFROTC; whether we received it; and, if we did, whether we could use it.

Table B.1. Scholarship Data Requested and Received

Data Requested	Data Received (yes or no)	If Received, Were Data Usable?
Was the cadet offered a scholarship? If so, did the cadet accept the offer?	No	N/A
Which type of scholarship program was the cadet offered (high school scholarship program, in-college scholarship program, etc.)?	Yes	No. Provided information on HSSP and ICSP scholarships, but did not provide information on scholarships for historically black colleges and universities or Hispanic-serving institutions, for example. Unable to verify accuracy of HSSP and ICSP data.
What type of scholarship was the cadet offered (type 1, 2, etc.)?	Yes	Not without significant cleansing; 8 percent of type-of-scholarship data were missing when years on scholarship data were available, and 20 percent of type-of-scholarship data were available, but years on scholarship were missing.
What was the dollar amount of the scholarship?	Yes	Yes.
What was the length of the scholarship offer?	Yes	Yes.
For how many years was the scholarship used?	Yes	Yes.
Were degree requirements attached to the scholarship offer (specific degree like electrical engineering, a technical degree, foreign language degree, etc.)?	No	N/A
Was the scholarship terminated because the cadet changed majors?	No	N/A
Was the cadet selected into the POC?	No	Obviously, cadets who were commissioned had been selected into POC. Other outcome variables (disenroll and dropped) do not provide information about POC selection.
Was the cadet commissioned?	Yes	19 percent of cadets on scholarship (years on scholarship > 0) had a missing outcome variable (dropped, disenrolled, or commissioned)

References

AFROTC—*See* U.S. Air Force ROTC.

Air Force Instruction 36-2640, *Executing Total Force Development*, December 16, 2008 (current as of December 29, 2011). As of March 9, 2015: http://static.e-publishing.af.mil/production/1/af_a1/publication/afi36-2640/afi36-2640_%28certified_current%29%29.pdf

Air Force Reserve Officer Training Corps Instruction 36-2011, *Cadet Operations,* August 12, 2013. As of March 9, 2015: http://www.citadel.edu/root/images/Airforce/AFROTCI36-2011_Aug_2013.pdf

Armacost, Andrew P., and James K. Lowe, "Decision Support for the Career Field Selection Process at the US Air Force Academy," *European Journal of Operational Research*, Vol. 160, No. 3, February 1, 2005, pp. 839–850. As of June 29, 2015: http://www.sciencedirect.com/science/article/pii/S0377221703005514

Ben-Tal, Aharon, Laurent El Ghaoui, and Arkadi Nemirovski, *Robust Optimization*, Princeton, N.J.: Princeton University Press, 2009.

Harrington, Lisa M., Lindsay Daugherty, S. Craig Moore, and Tara L. Terry, *Air Force-Wide Needs for Science, Technology, Engineering, and Mathematics (STEM) Academic Degrees*, Santa Monica, Calif.: RAND Corporation, RR-659-AF, 2014. As of February 16, 2015: http://www.rand.org/pubs/research_reports/RR659.html

Headquarters Air Force Personnel Center, *Air Force Officer Classification Directory (AFOCD),* Randolph Air Force Base, Texas: HQ AFPC/DPSIDC, April 30, 2013. As of March 9, 2015: http://www.uc.edu/content/dam/uc/afrotc/docs/UpdatedDocs2013/AFOCD_30Apr13.pdf

Jeanne M. Holm Center for Officer Accessions & Citizen Development, website, 2015. As of March 9, 2015: http://www.au.af.mil/au/holmcenter/

Lucia, Anntoinette D., and Richard Lepsinger, *The Art and Science of Competency Models: Pinpointing Critical Success Factors in Organizations*, San Francisco: Pfeiffer, 1999.

Parry, S. R., "The Quest for Competencies," *Training Magazine*, July 1996, pp. 48–56.

Taylor, Todd, "Bullet Background Paper on AFROTC Scholarships Meeting Air Force Requirements," AFROTC/RR, September 16, 2013.

U.S. Code, Title 10, Sec. 2107, Financial Assistance Program for Specially Selected Members, 2011.

U.S. Air Force, "United States Air Force Academy," fact sheet, August 18, 2004. As of January 16, 2013:
http://www.af.mil/AboutUs/FactSheets/Display/tabid/224/Article/104491/

U.S. Air Force ROTC, "Scholarship Types," web page, 2014. As of February 4, 2014:
http://www.afrotc.com/scholarships/types